with be

Mary Gladstone

"And there was the Cree, lying like a fat snake at the end of the field next to the double Dutch barn. When we first arrived, Mum warned us: the Cree was dangerous. If we trod on the mud we would sink without trace, and drown under the incoming tide. The river rose up in the hills but by the time it reached Carsenestock, it was wide, its bank sandy in places, muddy in others. Next to the sand and mud were 'the inks' or saltings: huge rectangles of grass like football pitches that flooded at high tide."

painting by David S. Gladstone

Jamie, Uncle Jim & Dad: David Gladstone

Siblings: Colin, Mary, & Lis Gladstone

San Francisco, Paris, Southerness, Washington, Santa Fe

THE MOSS OF CREE
A SCOTTISH CHILDHOOD

MARY C. GLADSTONE

firefall[tm]

For Julia Caird, my daughter & Julia Clarke, my friend

"There are impressions which neither time
nor circumstances can erase. Should I live
for centuries, the sweet period of my youth
would not be reborn, nor ever effaced from
my memory." *Jean-Jacques Rousseau*

First Edition: June 2018

hardcover: 9781939434487
paperbound: 9781939434555
ebook: 9781939434562
LC # tba

Paintings: David S Gladstone

Design & Editorial
Elihu Blotnick

FIREFALL EDITIONS
literary@att.net
Canyon, California 94516-0001
Galloway, Scotland DG9 9PU

www.firefallmedia.com

THE HIGHLAND SEA-tm
A FIREFALL ORIGINAL SERIES

Non-fiction Narratives
by Mary Gladstone

Largie Castle, a rifled nest
a search for self and family
1 (2017)

The Moss of Cree
A Scottish Childhood
2 (2018)

Inheritance
Glengarry Dragons
3 (2019)

INTRODUCTION

Mary as a wean

"DON'T PUSH IT!" She saw my finger on the buzzer. "Don't, Mary!"

But I did! Right away a man in uniform slid open the door and asked what we wanted. Mum said we didn't need anything. I only pushed the buzzer to see what would happen. It was close to my pillow. I was on the top bunk with no sheets, only blankets that scratched my legs. Near them was a red chain. Mum read out the notice beneath it. "Alarm. Pull the chain. Penalty for improper use £5." That was a lot! You could buy masses of things for that. Maybe a doll's house or even a bike. I wondered how many ice creams I might get for £5 and how much chocolate. It might fill two cupboards, at least.

It was one thing to push the buzzer but quite another to pull the chain. Mind you, I was strong enough to crack a nut by hitting it with a stone, step on a snail and break its shell, and even kick over a bucket in the stackyard, but I didn't think I could reach far enough to pull that chain. As for the buzzer, I could push it again and risk annoying Mum, but grabbing the chain and pulling it was something else. She would be furious and the man in the uniform might even throw me off the train. I tried to ask Mum what would happen if I did, but she was now feeding Janet her bottle, and Lis had begun to cry. Mum could read my mind anyway. She told me what would happen: the train would stop. "Just like that?" I asked. Mum nodded. I looked again at the chain and realised they were serious. At any rate, I'd have to give them £5. I didn't have that kind of money. I didn't have any at all.

"Go to sleep, Mary!" Mum ordered. "It's late and we've a long way to go." I laid my head on the pillow and tried to nod off but the train was too noisy. It banged and clanked when it did stop at a station, and as it pulled away, it gave a sudden jolt. The wheels didn't whisper or talk but shouted: "Go to sleep, little girl, go to sleep. Go to sleep, little girl. Sleep, sleep, sleep."

But I couldn't. Lis went out like a light as soon as Mum gave her a rusk. Janet was calm now that she was fed, but I was still awake. On curves and corners, the train swayed right over to one side. Helga, Mum's au pair, wasn't there to help. She had left two days before to go back to Switzerland where her family kept one cow, six chickens and a pig. For a goodbye, she gave me a costume, a big red skirt and a white blouse with yellow flowers sewn to the collar. Now Helga was gone, just like Anna and Martha before her.

They had come for a while, to help Mum change nappies, cook, clean, and take us for walks with Janet in the pram. They left and we never saw them again. But Dad hadn't left us. He went ahead of us, a week before Helga left in the opposite direction, so he could get our new house ready for us to move into.

When I saw him waiting there, I was happy and forgot about Helga, the nice quiet way she talked, and the old tree by the pond where she helped Mom lift me on to the back of Captain, a really big horse that pulled a cart and sometimes a plough.

"Look, children," announced Dad now, "have you ever seen a greenhouse? There's one here!"

A green house? I'd seen white houses; also cream, yellow, pink, and blue but never green. Did it have green windows and doors or green floors and ceilings? Maybe the bathroom was green, with towels, face cloth, bath mat, soap and toilet tissue to match. Green wasn't my favourite colour. I liked pink, then purple and last of all yellow, but green was alright. Better than a white house. White was boring. I was glad ours had color. We were at the back door where Mum had put out a bowl of water for our dogs, Breck and Bard. It was also where we kept our wellingtons and outdoor shoes so we didn't trail mud into the house.

"Come and see our new greenhouse!" Dad said again. He led us through the kitchen and along a passage until we reached a door into a room that was all glass, from top to bottom. Even the roof was of glass. "There you are! The greenhouse."

Dad looked proud. "When I was a boy I lived in a big house with a huge greenhouse, only we called it the conservatory."

"It isn't a green house." I was very disappointed. "It isn't green at all. It's a glass house."

"And people who live in them shouldn't throw stones!" Mum laughed.

"What do you mean?" I knew she was teasing me.

"Never mind!" she said.

Why was it called a green house, I wondered, when nothing was green about it at all? Mum and Dad were too busy to explain, but before they unpacked the plates, cups and saucers, stacked the pillows, sheets and blankets, hung pictures on the walls and organised the furniture, Mum gave Lis crayons to draw with, to keep her busy, and because I was older, she let me have a pot of red paint, a pot of blue and another of yellow. She also gave me a jar of water, a brush and six sheets of paper. Covering the first with red paint, I added some blue and it turned purple. I dipped the brush into the yellow, mixing it with blue and I'd got it. A lovely green.

And that's how I had the idea. I'd seen how people had come to our old house to paint the sitting room. I could do the same. I'd paint the greenhouse green.

"What on earth are you doing?" Mum asked.

I had just finished painting the nearest window but wasn't happy with the results. The colour was more like mud or dung than a proper green and it streaked. What was more, I was running out of paint. I'd used up all the yellow and most of the blue.

"Why did you do that?" Mum asked.

"I wanted a green house," I answered.

"Well, darling," Mum bent down to my level and took my hand in hers, "you can't always have what you want."

EXCEPT FOR THE SKY, all I could see from my bedroom window was the hill. I'd watch the clouds bounce off the top, which was low and round. The clouds were like torn bed-sheets as they sailed past until they reached another hill out of sight. Sometimes they hid everything but the bottomland and I'd imagine a giant had gobbled up the hill, believing it was a rock cake or bun. Sometimes the hill was green; then it turned purple, just like the blouse I wore on Sundays for church. Out of season the hill turned light brown with white around the edges, or it was white all over, but never a real white. I once heard Mum say the hill was speckly like a thrush's breast. It never got cold enough for deep snow here.

Often, before I went to bed, I'd look out and see the hill lit up with the sun sinking behind it like a red balloon. Other times, a dark patch rose slowly across it, reminding me of the shadow of a tiger in the jungle watching a deer, or a giant shark in the sea, its mouth open waiting to snap up fish in its jaws. I'd run to my bed, climb in and throw the blankets over my head, not waiting for Mum to say goodnight or tuck me up.

I liked the way the hill was so round, like Mum's breasts, which were big because she had three children now. Before she married they were quite small, she said. Most hills where we lived were not pointed. If you wanted those, steep and jagged, you had to go to Switzerland where Helga lived. Plenty were there. I preferred the hill across our river. One day, I would live on it, not by the river where we were. Half-way up my hill was a house, big and white with pillars at the front door. I wanted to know who lived there. Perhaps it was Cinderella's prince. Dad had read me a story about a young woman with a horrible mum and two nasty sisters, but the mum wasn't Cinderella's real mum and the sisters weren't her real sisters. Still, Cinderella tidied and swept up after them, never going out to play, unlike me who could do what I liked. In the end, explained Dad, Cinderella got her prince, just like I might if I played my cards right or, if not a prince, then a lord or a sir or if not one of these, a rich man.

I soon learned that an important lady lived in the house on the hill and when quite old, she learned to fly. She flew to England and over the sea, to Switzerland, and one day she left England to fly farther, perhaps even to America, and was never seen again.

I tried to see what else was on the hill. Mum had field glasses, a kind of telescope, only you looked through them with both eyes. She kept them to watch birds, which are harder than animals to see because flying is quicker than running. I asked to look through the glasses and Mum let me but I couldn't see the other airplane, the one that had crashed here in the war, flown by a pilot from Germany. Dad flew planes in the war too but over Italy, Sicily, and other ports. He said a lot of planes crashed, not just because people shot at them but their engines broke down or ran out of petrol. Then, like a bird killed in the air, the planes fell to the ground and sank or exploded just like that German one here. Dad said the man might not have known the hill was there and crashed because it was dark or foggy. Mrs. Erskine at Brown's told Mum that the man's family, his Mum, Dad and his sister, came from Germany every year to visit his grave, between Mr. Anderson and Mrs Howard in the churchyard.

"In death," said the Minister, "there's no difference between friends and enemies."

Dad never liked talking about the war. After all that scary night flying, his nerves got the better of him. I asked what he did when he flew near Italy, from Malta.

"I dropped bombs," he said, "and listened to the BBC and had a sing-song on the way home."

"What do bombs do when you drop them?" I asked.

"They blow up buildings like factories."

"Also houses and people," added Mum.

"And children and babies?" I asked.

"Let's change the subject," said Dad, clearing his throat.

"Yes, let's!" said Mum. "Would you like Welsh rarebit for tea, Mary?"

"No!" I thought Mum was pulling my leg. "I don't want to eat a rabbit. I like rabbits. I want to keep one in a hutch."

"Welsh rarebit is a rare, not often eaten meal," explained Mum, "it's delicious and special. It's really cheese on toast."

We always had cheese, milk, butter and even cream because Dad kept cows now: seventy altogether. They all gave milk but had no names. If a farmer had only one cow or possibly two, he gave them names like Daisy, Clover, Buttercup or Marigold. Dad couldn't work out what to call his cows, so he gave them numbers instead. He could have thought of names for twenty, but not all seventy. Mum said that, although the cows had no names, they were still important and should be treated well. I didn't like them; they were big and smelly and you couldn't ride them or give them a pat on their coat because dung was always coming out of their bottoms. To get me to like them better, Mum taught me this poem,

> The friendly cow all red and white
> I love with all my heart.
> She gives me cream with all her might
> To eat with apple tart.

The poem cow was friendly, but not ours. They weren't angry like bulls, that tossed you in the air, and I didn't love them, especially when they had no names. They gave you loads of cream but Dad didn't allow us to eat it; only the top of the milk for Sunday lunch when we had it with rhubarb tart.

> She wanders lowing here and there,
> And yet she cannot stray.
> All in the pleasant open air,
> The pleasant light of day.
> And blown by all the winds that pass,
> And wet with all the showers,
> She walks among the meadow grass
> And eats the meadow flowers.

The cows made a lot of noise, not lowing but bellowing when Bob Young took the calves away. I heard them from my bed. They bellowed all night. Mum tried not to say too much about it.

She explained that for us to drink milk and eat butter and

cheese, calves must be born so we can drink the milk for them. Bob's job was to take them from their mums as soon as they were born and drive them to the slaughter-house or put them in the calf shed where he fed them on a different kind of milk than their mother's. In winter, the cows stayed in the byre.

Bob fed them cattle cake and hay and mucked them out, and carried the dung in a wheelbarrow through the rubber swing doors to the midden. When the cows went out in the field, Mum could always tell; the milk tasted fruitier than when they were in the byre. Our fields had no flowers. Instead of buttercups and daisies, there was thick grass for the cows to eat so they would give gallons and gallons of milk.

Lots of visitors arrived on our doorstep; some invited, others not. I liked the wild geese that flew from Greenland and the north in squadrons, landing on the inks, which were grassy patches by the river. They came to feed and rest but weren't always treated nicely. Men with guns hung around waiting to shoot them.

The most important visitor was the milk lorry. It thundered down to the dairy where Bob Young helped heave the churns onto the back of the truck. After the lorry driver left Carsenestock, our dairy farm, he collected more milk from other farms on the Moss of Cree, before he headed for the creamery at Sorbie where the milk was made into cheese.

The person whose car Dad least liked seeing was the vet's. It cost a lot to call him out. He was a quiet man who stepped out of his car and, from the boot, lifted out his equipment, overalls and a pair of rubber gloves. With these, he entered the byre where, after inspecting the sick cow, he shoved his gloved hand and most of his arm into its bottom to find out what was happening to its unborn calf. If the vet's treatment was unsuccessful and the animal died, another visitor, Dundas Chemicals, the knacker, clattered down the road. Whenever we saw in the field a dead cow, its blown up body and four legs sticking up in the air, we knew the lorry would soon arrive, collect the dead animal, and leave with a tarpaulin spread over the body.

Like the wild geese, salesmen arrived without any warning too.

They entered by the back door and picked their way through slippers, wellingtons, dog bowls and coats until they reached Dad's office. They sold cattle cake, hay after a wet season, fence-posts, barbed wire, gates, tractors, combine harvesters, balers, mangers and water troughs, milking machines and livestock, from Friesian bulls to pullets. Dad kept his farming affairs a secret as he did not want us to know his business. What he earned and spent was nothing to do with us, he said.

As for the Inland Revenue, that was a foreign country as far as we knew. In any case, Dad hired an accountant to deal with such things. He could fly a plane and lead a squadron, but he wasn't handy about the house or farm and needed people to help him. He could draw plans for a house, and design greenhouses and up-stairs windows. He could even turn a loft into a studio but to do this he needed electricians, joiners, masons, builders, roofers, slaters and plumbers. On his own, Dad hardly knew how to change a plug himself.

One morning at breakfast-time, Dad said, "We've got a Queen now, not a King and she'll be crowned next week." He shoved his hand into his pocket and brought out a pencil sharpener and I could see the hole at the side where the point of the pencil was supposed to go in. It was a golden coach. "It's a model of the state coach the Queen rides in when she's crowned Queen Elizabeth the Second of England."

"And of Wales, Scotland and Northern Ireland," Mum added.

"Do you know how much the real coach weighs?" Dad asked as he handed me the pencil sharpener. "Four tons."

I tried to picture what else weighed four tons. An elephant? Whales, I knew were much heavier, especially blue ones. A bus was three times heavier than a coach because lots of people could fit in them. Only the queen and perhaps her family rode in a golden coach. Maybe it was as heavy as a tractor.

"It's so heavy that eight, white horses have to pull it and they always walk, never trot. And to stop it, a groom has to pull hard on the brake."

"They're not white but grey," Mum corrected him. "Windsor Greys, to be exact."

Inside the real coach, the Queen sits on a velvet seat and leans against satin cushions, but all I had inside my coach were pencil shavings. "Do you want to see the Queen?" asked Mum.

The Queen was visiting lots of towns in England and Scotland and was arriving on Tuesday in Newton Stewart, the town near where we lived. I wanted to see her and find out what she looked like, whether she was bigger or smaller than Mum and if she was older or younger. Mum drove me to Newton Stewart to the big square where lots of people stood and waited. In front of the crowd, a bench had been placed.

A lady told me to sit on it. She gave me a flag and told me to wave it as soon as the Queen arrived. Like Mum, the Queen had children. She had a boy, the same age as me, and a girl, a year older than Lis. The Queen's name was Elizabeth, her Mum was also called Elizabeth. Her Granny's name was Mary but she died not long ago. I asked if the Queen's children came with her when she visited. Mum shook her head. "They never go!" she said.

I felt sorry for them. When the Queen arrived and got out of her car, she looked too small to be a proper Queen and her coat and hat weren't pretty. I thought she would wear a long dress, a crown on her head, a sparkly necklace and hold an orb which is probably the most valuable ball you've ever seen with hundreds of precious stones on it and lots of pearls. I waved the flag at her.

Not long after the Queen's visit, I went to school for the first time and Mum bought me a school bag that was brown with two buckles in front and two long straps so I could wear it on my back. On the day before, she took me to the bottom garden where she grew carrots, lettuces and onions and told me to play on my own. She said she was tired and was feeling a bit queasy, because I'd soon have another sister, or brother. So, I played on my own but I wanted someone else to join in as Lis was too young. Just then, a girl came and stood outside the gate.

"Who are you?" I asked.

"Margaret!" she replied, and looked me in the eye.

"Look, I've got a new bag for school," I said.

"It's nice. I'll see you on the bus, tomorrow," she said.

But I didn't catch the bus. Mum drove me to school instead and, as we lined up in the playground, I noticed Margaret there. She came and stood beside me and stuck with me all day long. She sat in the next desk in class and went with me at lunch-time to the dining hall.

We had horrible stew with stringy meat and soggy carrots the size of our door-step. Pudding was worse. Yellow jelly with pretend cream, not like the stuff at home, which was thin, but still proper cream. As we left the hall, two big boys came up.

"You!" yelled the taller with red hair and a million freckles on his face, "Tell us something."

"Go on!" the smaller big boy giggled. "Jist talk! Tell us!"

I started to say the poem, the only one I knew by heart, about the friendly cow. I'd just got to the end of the second line when a stone hit me on my ankle. The taller boy threw it.

Margaret stepped in. "Stop that!" she yelled. "She's just a wean! I ken she's big but she's only wee!" The trouble was I was only five, but I looked older. Margaret was seven, almost eight, and she was the same size as me.

"I hate the bastard English!" shouted the red-haired boy.

"I'm not English," I said. "I'm Scottish."

"But ye talk like the English!" said the other one.

It was true I talked like the people at my old home in England. Even if I had changed how I spoke, would those boys be pleased? I wasn't sure. I wasn't like them. I didn't live in a house with a number like them. Mum and Dad didn't work for 'a boss' like theirs did either. Dad was 'the boss' and got people to work for him. I was different and they didn't like that.

I also never liked Mrs Gillanders, my first teacher. She got us to sit in this way: the cleverest at the back on the left. The next cleverest sat beside him or her. And so on until the dunce or the most stupid person sat at the front on the right. I never realised this all had to do with how important your dad was. At the top of the class was the boy with a policeman dad. The dad of the boy sitting beside him owned the shoe shop. I sat in the desk in front of them which meant I came third in the class.

First, we learned the alphabet, then we read sentences. By the time the teacher walked around giving out all the reading books, I had finished mine.

'Riting wasn't that easy because I was left-handed. Mum told Mrs Gillanders that she shouldn't make me write with my right because some people said it made you stutter. We didn't learn joined-up writing until we were older but it wasn't easy doing any kind. Even with ruled pages, I couldn't get my b's and p's to sit properly on the line. They ran up and down and all over the place. Eventually, I could do it, but only in Primary two.

'Rithmetic was awful. I could add up alright but taking away didn't work and I got in a terrible muddle. It didn't help when Mum and Dad told me that everyone in the family was hopeless at figures. "I could never do it!" said Dad. "I flew without instruments." But that didn't make sense. How could he do his sums for knowing how high up he was without being good at 'rithmetic? Dad designed houses as well and he had a measuring tape and special ruler to draw plans, so I'm sure he was good at 'rithmetic. He just said he wasn't.

Apart from 'riting and 'rithmetic Mrs Gillanders told us many stories, some frightening and some not so much. Aiken Drum was my favourite. It went like this: "There was a man lived in the moon, lived in the moon, lived in the moon. There was a man lived in the moon, and his name was Aiken Drum." After Mrs Gillanders in a funny voice recited this, we joined in with "And he played upon a ladle, a ladle and he played upon a ladle all day long." We did this often because there were lots of verses describing the man's clothes: his hat was of cream cheese, his coat of roast beef, buttons of penny loaves, waistcoat of crust pies, and breeches of haggis bags. I'd eaten haggis on Burns' Night. Dad brought it in from the kitchen on a big plate, cut it open with a knife, and recited a poem by Robert Burns praising the haggis.

Dad liked Robert Burns because he was a poet and a farmer

too and didn't like ploughing in the rain. Dad didn't like doing that either. The haggis tasted horrible, like meaty porridge. Mum told me what they put in it. "Awful offal," she said. "Sheep's hearts, blood and oatmeal and you wouldn't want to know what else! They put the whole mixture into a sheep's tummy and tie it up at the top."

Yuck! I liked Aiken Drum with his silly clothes of food even if they weren't my favourite. But why couldn't his hat be of dark brown fudge, yum, his coat of thick buttered toast, his buttons of chocolate wagon wheels, his waistcoat of custard creams and his breeches of omelettes or Mum's favorite, Welsh rarebit?

Dad liked me to eat a lot. Mum never forced me.

Not all Mrs G's stories were happy and funny. Some were extremely unfunny, and the story of Sawney Bean was really nasty; he lived, thank goodness, a long time ago, not that far from where my family was now in Newton Stewart. Sawney Bean stayed in a dark cave on the shore between Ballantrae and Girvan. I'd once gone to Girvan with Dad to buy six stirks from a farm near there. Stirks are bullocks between one and two years old.

Sawney Bean had fourteen children and also thirty-two grandchildren and for over twenty-five years, his family murdered as many as one thousand people. They would hide behind bushes and trees by the side of the road and jump out and kill people travelling to Glasgow or Ayr.

The poor people had no time to run away. The horrible Sawney, his sons and daughters, grandsons and grand-daughters, immediately set to cutting up the bodies, the sons and grandsons, sawing through the people's necks, waists and legs while the daughters and grand-daughters cut off the smaller parts like the person's arms, fingers and toes. When they were finished, they dragged back the cut-up parts to their cave, which at high tide was hidden from the road. Deep inside was a huge bucket of vinegar and they dropped the cut-up bodies into it to pickle them. When you pickle foods like onions, beetroot or cucumber, you can keep them for a long time before they rot. Mrs G said Sawney Bean and his family were very unusual. Very few people eat other people, but the Beans were cannibals, like on desert islands, where people, called natives, like to make meals out of people called missionaries, who come from countries like Britain, Germany, France, and America.

In the end, Sawney and his family were caught. At a fairground, probably in Girvan, they attacked a man carrying a pistol and he managed to escape. He reported the Beans to the Glasgow courts who told the King, who organised a big hunt with soldiers and hounds and masses of men with sticks, stones and swords. They hunted down Sawney, his children and grandchildren. Then, everyone lived happily ever after. They were no longer afraid to travel on the roads to Ayr or Glasgow. After a long trial with lots of people watching the Beans as they left the court-house, the family were hanged.

The real trouble was Mrs Gillanders scared me herself. When Billy Thompson threw a piece of scrunched-up paper at Johnny Miller, she pulled open the top drawer of her desk and took out her belt. "Hold out your hand!" she said to Billy; when he did, she hit it with the belt.

Billy wailed as he went back to his desk. Mrs Gillanders said he shouldn't make such a noise, he was a big boy now, and she had to punish him because she had to be cruel to be kind. Mrs Gillanders hit lots of us in Primary one for arriving late for class, for not bringing the correct dinner money, or not answering questions properly, or for talking when we weren't supposed to.

All the time I was in Primary one, I was terrified of getting the belt from Mrs Gillanders, so I behaved really well. The naughtiest boys didn't, but they didn't mind being strapped by her.

In Primary two, we had Miss Field, a nice teacher, who hardly ever strapped us. Because she never did, and we were used to Mrs Gillanders, who was so strict, we thought Miss Field was stupid being kind. Some boys played up and stuck chuddy, chewing gum under their desk lids and made faces behind her back when she wrote on the blackboard. Maybe because Miss Field was so easy, Margaret, who was still my best friend, went for a walk with me one lunch-time outside the school, down the road past the houses and shops, and past the shoppers on Queen Street, until we reached the square with the town hall on the other side. At the end of the town the farmers sold their cows and sheep at an auction market. We dashed into the building, built in a circle and saw young cows driven into a ring. Climbing to the top row of seats and looking down, we listened to the man below holding his hammer. "Twenty heifers from Baltersan. What am I bid? Twenty, thirty, forty, fifty. Fifty-five, sixty..." Still holding his hammer, the man banged it hard on the table and then started all over again. "Thirty Galloways from Grange of Minnoch. What am I bid? Twenty, thirty, forty, fifty-five, sixty..." Animals rushed in and out of the ring. Margaret and I couldn't keep count of them.

Margaret really didn't want to be bad and run away from school. "Come on!" I kept saying. Usually, it was she who made me be naughty, like in picking a red flower out of Mrs Black's garden up the road from where we lived. Once, we rang the bells of three houses and ran away before anyone had time to answer.

After we left the market, we were naughtier. We carried on more, down the road towards home. If I'd decided to go back then, I'm sure Margaret would've come, but she wanted to do what I wanted, so she followed. Maybe she still felt she should look after me, like she did on my first day at school. Lots of cars drove by, but nobody seemed surprised to see us alone without any grownup as we walked along the road. At the turn-off near the new houses, we saw Sheila Black's curtains move a little, but this frightening woman, who surely remembered when we stole her flowers, wasn't there. After two miles more, we were tiring, but just as we neared the Tile Works, we heard a car coming. As it approached, I saw it was a green pick-up van. I knew who was driving it.

"Here!" I grabbed Margaret's sleeve and pointed to a gate by the side of the road. "It's my Dad!" We climbed over the gate and hid behind the hedge. Afterwards, I left Margaret at her house and carried on walking until I reached the end of our road. I saw Mum standing by the stove at the kitchen window. She came out of the back door and said, "What on earth?"

Inside the kitchen, she offered me a glass of water. "You must be thirsty after all that walking!" She was angry but worried too.

"Why did you run away?" she asked.

I couldn't easily say. "I didn't feel well!" I explained.

"Have you a sore tummy?" Mum tried to work out what must be wrong. "A headache? Toothache, maybe? A sore finger? Possibly, a sprained ankle? What about a sore ear? You haven't been sticking anything in it, have you?" I could tell she didn't believe I was ill. She wasn't annoyed for long though and told me that I was a silly girl. The next day I caught the school bus carrying a letter from Mum to Miss Field. She didn't tell me what she had written but I guessed it was to ask the teacher not to be too hard on me as I was still very young. Margaret sat beside me but had no letter to give to the teacher.

Margaret's Dad Jimmy, worked for my Dad on the farm and because Jimmy had lots of children, he and his family had very little money. Some people said that Margaret's Mum couldn't read or write, so that's why she had no letter explaining why she ran away. When we entered the class, Miss Field did not look at all pleased and told us both off.

"We had three boys from Primary Five out on their bikes searching the countryside for you!" After staring at us angrily, she ordered me back to my desk but she made Margaret stand in front of the whole class and demanded she tell everyone why she had run away. Margaret refused to talk.

"Haven't you got a tongue in your head, Margaret Kyle? Well, if you've got nothing to say for yourself, I have!" Miss Field opened a drawer in her desk and got out her leather belt.

"Hold out your hand!" Margaret offered her right hand and down came Miss Field's belt, not once but three times.

It wasn't Margaret who wanted to run away. It was me; I'd got away with it while she took the blame. I felt bad.

And that was that. Margaret never spoke to me again. I missed our games of hopscotch. She called it peevers; with a piece of chalk we drew eight squares on the road outside the boiler house by the dairy and numbered them. Choosing a flat stone, we took turns to throw it on to a square, then hopped on to the others, avoiding the one the stone had landed on. On the way back, we picked up the stone from its square, making sure to avoid stepping on that space. I also missed picking rosehips at the end of summer. We brought them to school to be weighed by Mr Halliday, the head-teacher and he gave us 2d per pound. One year, I picked more rosehips than anyone else, so they gave me a badge.

When Margaret stopped sitting next to me in the bus, I wasn't sorry. Her coat and cardigan had an odd smell. Mum explained that, on wet days, the Kyles had nowhere except their living room to dry their washing. That was why her clothes smelled of coal fires and cooked food.

With no friends, I spent more time in my room. The hill was still there. I saw it through the clouds, when I looked out of the window, and thought of the important lady who flew off and was never seen again and the German who crashed into the hill in the war. I wondered how Dad had survived while the German was killed. One day, I decided, I would climb that hill and find the wrecked plane. Dad knew what it was like to fly in bad weather and told us how he fought the wind, rain and the enemy too.

While we were at the table one evening, he got up and brought back a special piece of broken wood to show us. "Here it is!" he said, lifting a piece of airplane propeller. "I flew into a power line," he laughed. "Do you know, I've crashed three airplanes! Look!" He opened an album with photographs showing heaps of wood, canvas, metal and a wing that looked as if it belonged to a gigantic bird. "I was lucky", he had written under the first photograph. "Yes" under the second, and "Very" under the third.

"Was this before the War began?" I asked. Dad nodded and flashed me a smile. "At Cambridge, where I learned," he said.

Lis, Janet and I flew too. In our imaginations we soared to the tops of the firs in the wood near the Tile Works at Carty port. We also played in the barn where Dad stored bales of hay and straw. We found wheat sheaves stacked by the door. Grasping one, I rode it like a witch her broomstick, jumping off a pile of bales to land in the hay. The other side of flying was falling.

Mum and Dad had a set of table mats with pictures by an artist called Breughel. One mat showed harvesters taking a rest in a corn-field. The others were of children in a playground, hunters in the snow, and guests at a wedding feast. The last had a man ploughing a field by the sea and out of the sky was another falling into the water. So, that was that. When you flew, you could just as easily fall to the ground as soar to the stars.

I still missed Margaret but she stayed away. Lis and Janet played with each other and made friends with Anne and Gladys Young, our neighbors. Sometimes I helped Mum in the garden. Even if I had wanted to, Dad would never have allowed me in the byre or dairy. Even the boiler house was forbidden. This was where Bob Young washed the churns, pipes, buckets and fingers he attached to the cows' udders at milking time. But Mum and Dad let me go to the field when they made hay. Dad phoned the weather station for a forecast, before they began.

"No point in cutting hay in a downpour," he announced.

First, Jimmy drove to the field on the tractor; after he cut the hay with the binder, it lay out for a day or two to dry. He returned with the baler which scooped up the hay and chucked it out in square blocks all over the field.

When rain threatened, everyone helped and Mum drove one of the tractors. We had a red one and 'a wee grey Fergie'. The men loaded the trailers, when the bales were heavy, piling them one on top of the other, five or six layers high. When they took a break, Mum went back to the house to make tea, pouring it into thermos flasks to keep it warm. I helped make cheese and ham sandwiches. Together, we carried the food and tea in a picnic basket down to the field. When the hay bales were ready to come in, Jimmy lifted me on to the top of them, just like Wilkie on our farm in England had got me to sit on the old cart-horse. This was what I had been waiting for, to ride on the bales, to seize a branch of the ash tree as the trailer went by, swinging from side to side, its tires bouncing off the rough track when it dipped into the hollow by the gateway, then rose again at the top of the slope. More helpers waited at the hayshed: Mrs Young and one or two of Jimmy's older children, but never Margaret. She stayed at home with Mrs Kyle. In the shed the boys and men worked as a team, pressing tightly together the bricks of hay, some flat or upright and others at a slant so they fitted into each corner of the barn.

One morning, a tall man appeared at the back door. This was Snib Scott, who held a stick in one hand and an old Ministry of Food's National Dried Milk can in the other. As he walked down the road, he would stop at each farm and demand food and drink. This time, after banging on our back door with his stick, he sat down on the bank under the ash tree.

Mum, who was preparing sandwiches for the hay-makers, came out to see who it was and groaned when she saw Snib.

"I'll tak' a cup o' tea, Mrs!" Snib said. It was an order rather than a request. Unused to such treatment, Mum was stunned into complying. "An' a piece while you're at it," he added. "White pan loaf wi a wee bit Tate & Lyle golden syrup." Although Mum's service was prompt, Snib sent back the tea. "It's no sweet enough. I sez three, no twa spoons, Mrs!"

At that moment, Dad appeared. Looking up at the sky, then at Snib, his legs spread out before him. "You're just the man I'm looking for, Mr Scott!" Dad said.

No stranger to mockery, Snib wasn't amused by my father's way of addressing him. "If you would be good enough to help with the hay, you can have a slap-up meal on the house!" said Dad.

Snib gave no answer.

"Roast beef, new potatoes, peas! Cheese, bread, the lot!"

"A canny work on an empty stomach. A'll hae to eat afore I work!"

"Alright, Snib. We'll see what we can do."

Five minutes later, Mum brought him a tray laden with food.

Accepting it, the tramp tucked in and when he finished, he stood up, burped and made for the back door.

When it opened, Mum and Dad stood there, expecting Snib to accompany them to the field. "Are you ready?" asked my father.

Snib shook his head. "If a man canny work on an empty stomach, he canny dae it on a full yin either." Grabbing his stick and tin, he disappeared up the road.

Initially affronted, Mum was amused by Snib's cheek and the incident became a conversation-piece at her next dinner party. "Not only did he refuse to work after we fed him but he sent back the tea in that horrid old tin of his, saying it wasn't sweet enough!"

"Ridiculous!"

"Unbelievable!"

"Who is he?"

"No-one knows. Some say he may be the illegitimate son of a baronet."

"He's certainly got airs..."

"and graces..."

"Others say he is a cashiered serviceman."

"Or a war hero with a military cross won in the desert with Monty but, after the war, he couldn't adapt to civvy street."

One guest told Mum that Snib lived with the tinkers at The Gass, a farm in the hills above Newton Stewart.

Identifying tinkers with Tinkerbell, the fairy in 'Peter Pan', I saw Snib, who would sooner curse or throw stones at us, as a gnarled goblin, not a fairy.

At harvest-time, the procedure was much the same as when making hay. Jimmy cut the barley with the binder. Then he drove Dad's red tractor, a Massey Ferguson, which pulled the combine harvester, a colossal machine stored in the double Dutch barn beside the midden.

To me, the combine was a greedy monster but Dad thought it magical, the way it separated grain from chaff.

I'd already heard about grain and chaff at Sunday School. Our teacher said they stood for two kinds of people and the way they behaved. She advised that our lives should be like grain, not chaff.

Jimmy steered the tractor and Dad stood on a platform in the centre of the combine, checking that the grain fell correctly from the chute into a sack. After that job was over, the baler swept up the straw from the ground and baled it. Everyone helped to bring it in, only this time it wasn't urgent. It was a pity if the straw spoiled but it wasn't a disaster; straw was for bedding, not fodder.

Dad liked haystacks and wheat-sheaves because they looked nicer than bales of hay or barley. When he first started farming with a horse-drawn reaper, he never dreamed of owning a combine harvester. He loved machines like airplanes, motor boats, cars and tractors but he never knew how to mend them when they refused to work. He got someone else to do that.

One late afternoon, when Dad and Jimmy were out in the field by Kelly port, the combine harvester broke down.

"Damn!" Noticing clouds dance over the top of the hill, Dad was worried. "Why won't the bloody thing start?" he asked.

"I dinny ken, man!" answered Jimmy as he poked his nose into the threshing section, the grain chute, and sack. Dad was furious. It wasn't clear if he was more annoyed with Jimmy or the combine harvester. He shoved his right hand deep into the machine and a large, canvas belt suddenly sped into motion taking off the top part of his index finger and a slice off its neighbour. Lis, Janet and I knew nothing about the accident until tea-time when we came in from the barn where we had been playing.

"Daddy's in bed," Mum announced. "He's not very well," she said, handing each of us cheese on toast and a glass of orange juice. She switched on the television and told us to watch 'Crackerjack!'. I knew something wasn't right as she never plonked us in front of the TV, like Dad did. Instead, she got us to read a book or play cards. "What's wrong with him?" I asked.

"He's hurt his finger...with the combine harvester. The doctor's come and given him something for the pain and told him to stay in bed."

"Is it sore?" asked Janet.

"Yes. Very," Mum answered.

As Lis and Janet sat glued to the TV screen, I climbed the stairs and stood on the landing outside Mum and Dad's bedroom. I dared not enter as Mum had warned me not to, but the door was open and I could hear Dad moaning inside. What I heard was a lot of whimpers followed by a long groan. I crept away silently.

After Dad's accident, he stayed inside. After lunch he went into our 'good' sitting room, which Lis, Janet and I didn't enter except on special occasions like Christmas, birthdays and cocktail parties. He had bought a radiogram so he could listen to 33 rpm records. When he played them we could hear men and women singing, through the closed door. The women's voices sounded like runny honey and the men's like neighing horses. The women sang very high, but not so high that only a dog could hear them.

I wasn't used to women expressing themselves so noisily. Mum almost never did. She was very reserved. I'd never heard her so much as sing the national anthem or 'auld lang syne' at the end of a party. She didn't hum tunes either. If she ever sang, at church, she was like a set of bagpipes, her drones making monotonous moans. The women who sang on Dad's records were like deer, bolting into the trees, leaping across heather, suddenly halting, then running up and down scales like a person darting up and downstairs.

"Callas is the best!" said Dad. Her voice carried you to a vast heaven where you floated on clouds like the ones I watched from my bedroom window. "What a voice Callas has!" Dad said.

I didn't understand. Mum explained, callous was when, for no reason at all, a person killed a mouse poking its head out from behind a barley stalk. On the other hand, a callus could be a thick, hard patch on your foot. However, Dad meant Callas, the famous Maria Callas, the greatest soprano in the world.

One day Lis and I took a walk past the dairy and small byre. Beyond them, through an archway, was the calf shed and, at the far corner of a yard, the steps to the granary. On the ground, to the left was the engine shed of black corrugated iron. Inside were oil drums, old tractor tires, a rusting outboard motor, twine, rolls of barbed wire, fence posts, a broken plow blade, and a harrow. Jimmy sat on an upturned oil drum, eating his piece, one of spam, the other of jam. "Hello, Jimmy!" I said. He smiled at me, then pulled a scary face.

"I'm no Jimmy Kyle. Do ye no ken who I really am? I'm Sawney Bean! Do ye ken what he did?" He unbuckled the leather belt around his waist and took a lunge, pretending to hit us with it. We ran and hid round the side of the shed. Returning a few minutes later, we heard him announce, "Sawney ate weans for his tea, so he did!" Jimmy took another swipe at us, pretending to be a monster. We screamed and ran back to the house.

Since Jimmy and Mrs Kyle had ten children, it was quite a squash for them to live in a little cottage with only two tiny bedrooms. Margaret wasn't the oldest, nor the youngest. Coming in somewhere in between, she had an older brother, about thirteen years old, called Rab but he wasn't like other boys of his age. He spoke slowly, as if he couldn't find the right words. He was difficult to understand. He would come to our farm looking for work and sometimes Dad got him to paint a shed or bring the cows in from the field for milking. When Bob Young went to Arbroath for a fortnight's holiday, Dad let Rab help in the byre. For three days the cows produced eight more gallons yield. Dad was delighted. He thought it might be down to Rab's special way with animals, until one day on entering the dairy, Dad saw Rab, hose in hand, watering the milk.

"What on earth?" Dad was horrified,when the lad announced, "I thought you'd like when I did that, Mister!" Dad waited for the balloon to go up, for the creamery to tell him they no longer wanted his milk. But no phone call or letter came. "Luckily we got away with it!" he whispered to Mum, who was making a cheese sauce on the electric cooker in the kitchen. "If we had been found out, that would have been it," he declared. For those caught watering their milk, a crime no dairy farmer in his right mind would commit, it meant closure and certain bankruptcy.

Every farm had to accept a visit from the milk recorder who was feared, like all health inspectors who arrived unannounced to make spot checks. Mike was our first recorder; he disliked children and made us nervous by joining us at our evening meal and staying over-night so he could rise in time to inspect the early morning milking. Sheila, the next recorder, was nicer. Once, she arrived on Christmas Eve as Willie Paterson, the grocer, drew up in his van. After Mum bought 2 lb sugar, ½ lb butter, and a packet of fruit gums for us to share, Sheila stepped up to Willie's counter and chose three Cadbury's Selection boxes as presents for Lis, Janet and me.

"Aren't you going home for Christmas?" I asked.

"No! I work at Christmas! Cows don't get the day off, do they?"

I knew that, come what may, cows were milked daily but did the milk recorder have to work too?

"I like my work," said Sheila.

"You're a true Calvinist!" Dad declared as he slopped three large spoonfuls of shepherd's pie onto her dinner plate. "And there's nothing wrong with that," he added, not wanting to offend her. "Help yourself to Birds' Eye garden peas," said Dad, stressing the word on the frozen pea packet telling an outright lie.

Although Dad stopped Rab from working in the dairy, he still visited us. One afternoon, he approached Lis, Janet and me. We were in the yard opposite the back door of our house. "Come wi' me," he said to me, "an' I'll give ye six pens!"

I was a bit tempted. To have, not one pen but six, was terrific. However, I couldn't see how Rab, who had nothing, not even a proper coat or bike, had six pens. What was more, why would he want to give them to me? Pens, crayons and pencils were what I liked. For my birthday, I'd asked for a set of coloured pencils and sure enough, I got them. They were Lakeland pencils and came in a rainbow of colours: from primrose yellow to dark gold and rose pink to deep crimson.

The next day, Rab returned and I asked if he had brought the pens he had promised. I had thought about them all day. I wondered what they would look like. I knew you could buy different kinds of pens. Mum had even shown me a quill, made from a crow's feather. "That's what they wrote with in the old days," she said. Dad already had a new kind of pen called 'The Jotter', which had a metal ball covered with ink at its point to write with. At school, but not until we were in Primary three, we wrote with a pen that had a metal nib. At the front, right-hand corner of our desks, was a china well filled with ink and, after every three or four words, we dipped our pen nibs into it for more.

"Where are the pens?" I asked. Rab looked at me as if I was mad. "Here it is!" He handed me six pence. "There's yer six pence! Now, come wi' me," Rab said.

We followed him past the dairy, through the archway by the calf shed and across the yard to the bottom of the stairs and up to the granary. At the top was a door with an iron handle, very stiff to turn. Rab took a hold of it and pulled the door open, its bottom scraping the floor-boards. The granary was on two levels, the upper part reached by steps. It was empty, but still smelled fusty. The far end was open so you could look down on to the tractors parked below.

Rab told my sisters to go away. He grabbed my hand. "Here!" he pointed to an empty sack on the floor. "Lie down on that there!" I never thought to say no. I did what older people told me usually and Rab was almost grown up, so I lay on the sack and, as he unfastened the fly of his trousers, he told me, "This is what they do, yon big folk. I seen it."

I heard a loud noise outside, then the sound of someone climbing the stairs, and the door swung open.

Mum told me to sit in the waiting room while she spoke to the doctor in his surgery. I tried out two or three chairs, then sat on one beside a table piled with magazines. A woman smiled at me from the top cover. Mum hadn't explained why she brought me here. We hardly ever visited the doctor. Often, he came to us.

He'd follow Mum up the stairs, through the narrow passageway, until he discovered the bedroom where his patient lay. On his instructions, we'd open our mouths and say AAAAAh, let him hear our chest with his stethoscope, and answer his questions, like do you see double? Have you been sick? Can you touch your toes? After his examination, we'd always receive a clean bill of health. So, why had Mum brought me here now, when I wasn't feeling ill? My tummy didn't hurt, neither did my head. My back felt fine. I wasn't sick.

I looked up and saw through the window one of the doctor's sons kicking a ball outside. It was Patrick, who was quite tall for his age. Seeing him reminded me of when he and his brothers spent the afternoon at Carsenestock, my farm. We played a rough game of tig. We all rushed up the front stairs, through two bedrooms and down the back stairs, until Patrick's older brother, Christopher slammed a door on Lis' finger, and Mum had to phone the boy's father to ask if he could attend to her injured child. The doctor's boys never came to our house again.

After a while, Mum came out of the surgery and the doctor asked me to enter on my own.

It was a long, narrow room. He sat at a desk. Around his neck hung a stethoscope. I noticed a set of weighing scales on the floor. The doctor stood and drew back a curtain to his examination room and told me to climb up onto a high, narrow bed but he didn't examine me there...

After school, Lis and I ran down to the engine shed to be scared by Jimmy again. Maybe he'd pull a frightening face, play the ogre or the terrifying Sawney Bean. I liked him doing that. I enjoyed pretending to be afraid; running away, hiding for a few moments, then returning. He finished tidying his tools on the work-bench and was about to sweep up, when we arrived.

"Hello, Jimmy!" I called.

No answer.

"Hello, Jimmy!" Lis said.

He stopped sweeping and suddenly hissed like a snake. "Get the hell out of here!" he yelled.

For a few moments I thought he was joking and I giggled.

"Do ye hear me?" he unfastened his belt and holding it by the buckle, he threatened us with it, shouting, "I'll leather ye!"

We ran away.

WHAT MADE JIMMY so angry and why did he want to hit us? This time, he meant to. He wasn't pretending. Was it to do with Rab and me in the granary? Was I bad? Really bad? Because Mum and Dad weren't talking to me now.

But it wasn't my fault. How was I to know that Rab would get me to do that, and what was that anyway? Nobody would say. I could not ask Mum and Dad; they refused to discuss it. After Jimmy and his family left, the Kyles were never spoken of again and I had no idea where they went. Soon afterwards, another man called Tony, came to work on the farm. He had a wife and two girls who never visited us, far less offered us money to go with them to the granary.

I often stayed in my room and looked out of the window. As clouds sailed by, I imagined riding on them, flying to a country with wooden houses built on hills with pointed, snowy tops; in the fields were cows with clanking bells around their necks.

But I wasn't there; I was here living by a river next to many bellowing cows and a droning milking machine.

On the other hand, I no longer had to bump into Margaret sulking on the school bus. However, I still felt bad. But I was sure I wasn't. Sometimes, I wondered, though. Dad wouldn't talk about it, nor would Mum ever. All she did was drive me to the doctor but he had said nothing either.

I had my own room but Lis and Janet shared theirs.

At bed-time, Dad would tell them a story to help them go to sleep. "Once upon a time, there were two boys," he would begin.

I heard shrieks of laughter. "Sit still, Janny, and listen," Dad said, "and Lis, concentrate! This is a very important story! The boys were called Johnny and Tommy."

"Johnny and Tommy! Johnny, Tommy! Johnny and Tommy!"

I could hear the bedsprings creak as my sisters jumped up and down on their beds. "Stop it, you naughty girls and listen! Now, Johnny was walking along the road as happy as a lark..."

"What's a lark, Daddy?" asked Lis.

"A silly bird that sings in the sky! When, what did he see?"

"Well, what?" Janet was impatient.

"A blackbird flying upside down and doing slow rolls at the same time!"

"Birds don't fly upside down," said Lis.

"You're right," admitted Dad. "They don't do slow rolls either. Only airplanes can do that! Now!" Dad began his story again. "Johnny and Tommy had been working hard in the hay-field and they were very hungry. They came to an inn..."

"What's that?"

"A kind of hotel where they serve food, and they asked for lunch...And, do you know what the fat old woman gave them?"

"What?"

"What?"

"You won't believe it, she brought them a huge pot of mutton broth,"

"Mutton broth?"

"But it wasn't that; it was nose blow, snails, Breck's sick, dead spiders and bats' wings."

"Oh, yuck, yuck, yuck..."

Sometimes the stories had better endings. Tommy feasted on ice cream, chocolate and trifle. Johnny rode wild horses and got thrown off, or the boys shot towards the stars in a special rocket.

I could hear Dad and my sisters in the other room but I never joined in. "Go to sleep, Mary, you're too old for Johnny and Tommy stories," Dad shouted.

I returned to my bed, telling myself I didn't need them or their stories and what was more, I didn't want them. Neither did I want Dad or Mum to tuck me up. For that matter, I didn't want anyone to do it. I could manage on my own.

I didn't see much of Mum now. She was there at breakfast-time but not often at lunch. When I asked where she was, Dad told me that she was unwell. After tea, one evening, when Lis and Janet were in the greenhouse picking tomatoes, taking care not to pull them too hard in case the plant stems broke, I heard Dad speaking on the phone. "How can we afford another," he said, "especially if it's a girl. Three are enough!"

Since Helga left, Mum had nobody to give her a hand in the house. So, Dora came. She lived in a village by the sea. Her Dad was a fisherman. Dora had short brown hair and wore beige overalls so her clothes didn't spoil when she was cleaning the house. "Your Mum isn't strict," she told me on her third day. "Not like mine. She'd sooner skelp than praise us!"

"What did she skelp you for?" asked Lis.

"Spilling water on the table, getting grease on my peeny, or tearing my clothes. We were to be a' neat and tidy: collars clean, cuffs straight, clothes ironed, no loose buttons, straight hems. She was a real stickler, my Mum. But you could eat your dinner off her front door step, it was that spick and span."

Dora liked everything Scottish and little that was English. Scots were braw, which meant brave, wonderful or extraordinary and if your jumper or scarf was especially nice, it was 'braw' too. Sometimes her Scottish likes and English hates were too much, making me want Helga back. But Mum said she was done with the Swiss, their 'ferocious cleanliness' and cuckoo clocks, but I missed the way Helga put me on her knee and sang me nursery rhymes.

She would describe what her country was like. "Switzerland is divided into four parts: the German, French, Italian and Romansh. It's a bit like when you cut an apple in four."

"Four parts?"

"Four quarters," Helga insisted on using correct English. She loved telling me about William Tell, who refused to bow to the town's mayor. To punish him he forced Tell, to shoot an apple on the top of his son's head. Luckily, he could hit anything. His first arrow split the apple in half without touching a hair. I wondered how anybody could aim so straight? We tried it with our dartboard. Mum made sure there were no apples lying around. "We don't want you killing each other," she said.

Mostly we argued about toys. One day, Lis claimed Heather, my Scottish doll, was hers. Dad gave us dolls for our birthdays and for my fourth, he bought me a set of four: an English one called Rose, with pink cheeks, blue eyes and what Dad called, flaxen hair; Heather who had dark brown hair, wore a floppy bonnet, and a black and green tartan kilt; Myfanwy, the Welsh doll wore a red apron over a long, black dress and on her head a tall black hat; and Colleen, from Ireland with red hair and a green dress. Since I painted the greenhouse, I wasn't keen on green any longer, so Colleen was now my least favourite. Mum was unimpressed by Dad's choice of presents. "I never had dolls. Sticks and stones and animal bones were good enough for me. I played with them all day long."

But I wasn't Mum, so Helga kept the peace. Soon after Dora arrived, I saw Mum packing a case in her bedroom.

"Where are you going?"

"To hospital!"

"Why?"

"To have a baby!"

"Another one?" I hadn't noticed her tummy getting bigger. She spent little time with me except to help with my homework.

Dora made up for Mum's absence. She had us playing hide and seek so every corner of our house became familiar to us: from our 'good' sitting room, that had a press of latticed glass doors and on the shelves three pieces of Venetian glass and a cracked Wedgewood bowl, to the front bedroom with its sloping ceiling and dormer window. Sometimes we hid behind a large bookcase or in another room where we watched television, or in the dining room next to the kitchen, or any corner we could find upstairs. When it was Dora's turn to catch us, she would warn that she was coming by shouting, "Fee, fie, foh, fum, I smell the blood of an Englishman. I'm coming to get you. Just you. Grrrrrrr!"

The growl showed Dora meant business. She left nothing to chance, turning over cushions and peering beneath chairs and sofas. Upstairs, she hunted under beds and even stripped them in case someone was hiding under the blankets. She ransacked cupboards: larder, boot-hole, dog store, coal-house and greenhouse. There was only one place she didn't bother with. Behind a door on the landing was an awkward space, and to enter it, you crawled on hands and knees along loose floor-boards. Low and narrow, it was not big enough for grownups to tackle. This tunnel led to a larger space where chairs with broken seats, trunks full of Dad's old papers, Christmas decorations and Halloween costumes were stored. We hid here because we knew Dora wouldn't follow. When she failed to find us, she opened the door on the landing and yelled, "Alright, you lot. I ken fine you're in there. Out now! It's past your bed-times!"

Our consolation while Mum was away were the grocers' vans who visited. The fishmonger only came every other Wednesday as Mum wasn't overly fond of fish, and Dad preferred the butcher next to Newton Stewart market.

On Tuesdays, Mr Drem would arrive after Mum phoned in her order but while she was in hospital, Dora took charge. Mrs Drem would weigh the tea, coffee, sugar and flour and pour them into brown paper bags, closing them with an origami-like fold. Sometimes Mum became suspicious and as soon as Mr Drem departed, she brought out her kitchen scales and weighed each item. "Just checking! These two pound bags of sugar are incredibly light," she would say.

Late on Saturday afternoon, a second grocer visited: Willy Paterson from Kirkcowan, a village situated close to the Stranraer road. He drove a dark blue van, a grocer's show-case, acquired for his rural sales. Demonstrating his allegiance to the workers, he'd visit the Youngs first. To view his merchandise, Mum climbed several steps to arrive at his fold-away counter, where he stood in brown overalls. He was always obliging particularly in the run-up to Christmas and New Year when customers splashed out.

"Is it drinking chocolate or cocoa, Mrs Gladstone?" he would ask. "What does the recipe say? Half a pound of butter! Sure that's enough with your growing brood?" and he winked at Janet who clutched the hem of Mum's skirt. "How are you off for New Year...I mean Christmas?" He remembered to correct himself, knowing not to mention only the pagan festival. He must have got wind that we were either English or non-Presbyterian and likely to regard the Christian as more important.

Most people in Wigtownshire in the Fifties ignored Christmas;

both Bob Young and Jimmy worked on the day. "I've got currants, sultanas, raisins, suet, marzipan, icing sugar, oh, and eggs, flour, self-raise of course, and baking powder." The list tripped off his tongue as fast as the auctioneer encouraging bids for cattle at the market. Mum kept her distance giving Willie Paterson a look that was meant to show she was nobody's fool, least of all his, but too often the grocer's calculations, worked out on a carbon pad with a picture of a fat man in an apron, carrying a box laden with ham, oranges, cheese and batons of bread, confused her; arithmetic was not Mum's strong point either.

While Mum was in hospital, a more exotic salesman came to the door: a Sikh in a turban. He drew up in a white van packed with stoles, scarves, and bolts of cloth that shone and shimmered. On the ground, he laid out candles, incense, perfumes, pendants, carved soapstone, bangles, and more cheap-looking jewellery. Mum did not like to encourage such people, referring to them as pedlars but since she wasn't at home to object, Dad had few qualms. "How much is that?" he asked, pointing at a scarlet stole in wild silk.

He wanted it for Mum. Whether he bartered for the stole or not, I don't know but he bought it nonetheless, and Mum wore it for each Pony Club Christmas dance we attended.

After three days she returned. Dad fetched her from Stranraer hospital. She stood at the back door beside the wellingtons and the table where the postman placed the mail. In her arms was a baby. Lis, Janet and I stretched on tip-toe to see it. "Careful!" Dad said. "This is Colin, your brother!" and, under his breath he muttered, "Our long-awaited boy!"

Colin attracted much attention; telegrams arrived from aunts, uncles and cousins with a variety of messages: "So glad you have your boy at last!" and "Excellent! A son and heir!" Mum mixed Colin's Formula milk with extra care, as she didn't breast-feed us.

As if to take revenge on their ungrateful parents, Janet and Lis reacted strongly. One morning after breakfast, Janet followed Dad to the double Dutch barn by the midden. He loaded hay bales on to the trailer and started up the tractor engine. When it reversed, one bale fell off on to Janet, who fell to the ground and hit her forehead on a stone, that cut and bloodied her face. She needed stitches. Mum rushed her to the doctor. The next day, not to be outdone, Lis stretched up towards the cooker in the kitchen and pulled a pot of boiling water over her hands and right arm. "Oh, dear!" Mum said after the mishap. "My daughters' noses have really been put out of joint!" My Mum wasn't speaking literally, but she could have been. Not until Janet was eighteen did anybody guess that the bale that hit her had also broken her nose.

Dora shoved us aside. That was the hardest part of having a baby brother. Gone were our rowdy games like 'tig' on the tarmac outside the boiler house or hunts for four-leafed clovers along the farm road. Hide and seek games ended too. When Mum and Dad went to a cocktail party or Dad attended a church vestry meeting while Mum was at the WRI, the Women's Rural Institute, Dora had encouraged us to play our games. Now she ordered us to watch television: instalments of 'Billy Bunter', the fat schoolboy. Lis and Janet settled for 'Watch with Mother'. Dora was ecstatic about Colin. His brown eyes were a novelty to her and everyone else. They were like Mum's, a Celt through and through. We three sisters took after Dad whose eyes were cobalt blue. Dora cooed over our brother. "Who's my wee boy, then?" she'd say, chucking him under his chin. "Who, then?" she shook her head from side to side and made a funny face, stuck out her tongue, and tugged at the skin beneath her eyes to look like a blood-hound. Her expressions were much like the faces Jimmy pulled in the engine shed. Being reminded of him made me uncomfortable. Dora also made baby noises for Colin's benefit. "Bur-bur-bur-bur-ba! Who's my wee boy, then?" She'd grasp Colin under his arms and lift him toward the ceiling. "He's my wee boy, is he no? That's right. You get they sisters into line! You're the wee man o' the house now, are you no? Ay, you're the wee boss!"

Many people admired our brother, paid their respects, and congratulated Mum for producing a boy. The first to visit was 'The Major' or Michael Cliff McCulloch, who farmed Carse of Clary at the other end of the Moss of Cree, which was nearly impossible to cross. Michael once tried to take a short cut to Carsenestock over the Moss but ended up in a ditch. This wouldn't have been a problem for a fit man but, ever since we knew him, Michael was confined to a wheel-chair. As a 26 year old soldier during the war and stationed in Iran, he was struck down by polio. Waking one day, he found himself paralysed and was rushed to hospital. Doctors saved his life but he never regained the power of his legs and the strength of his arms and chest was very much weakened.

Michael visited us on Sunday afternoons in a motorized three-wheeler. To keep his legs dry, he covered them with an oiled cloth and his dog accompanied him. He kept a series of Alsatian bitches. Whereas Heidi was gentle; her predecessor, Brunhilde was not. Michael warned us not to touch her.

Michael's chariot was too wide to pass through our back door. The only way he could enter the house was to manoeuvre his vehicle into our greenhouse. It was here, when Colin was a new-born, that Michael was introduced to his godson. "I might drop him!" Michael chuckled after Dad thrust the noisy bundle into his arms. Positioned beside the tomato plants and greenfly, he quickly relinquished Colin to Mum. Accepting a cup of tea and a slice of christening cake, Michael asked Dad how well the grass in the fields he had limed was growing.

Unable to walk, Michael enjoyed speed, like my Dad. Apart from attending the races in Ayr and playing a mean game of Bridge, Michael drove a Bentley with hand controls and sped around the country in it with Heidi perched on the back seat. To reach Michael's house we had to drive to 'the new houses' and turn left on to the main Newton Stewart-Wigtown road.

I was in Primary three now. Mrs Dunlop, my new teacher, curious about my baby brother, ordered me to stand in front of the class and give information about him. She battered me with questions. "What's the baby's name?" she enquired.

Dissatisfied by my answer, she demanded I tell her more. "Surely he has more than one name! What is it?"

"Hew," I replied.

"How do you spell it?" Mrs Dunlop realised that my brother's second name was an opportunity for a spelling lesson. She moved to the blackboard, picked up a piece of chalk and inscribed the names, 'Hew' and 'Hugh'.

"A boy," she explained "can be called 'Hew' or 'Hugh'. Mary's Mum and Dad have chosen the spelling of the former. In short, they call him 'Hew'," she said, tapping the board with her chalk.

Mrs Dunlop wasn't going to let me off easily; she had tons of questions. "How much does your brother weigh?" she demanded.

I didn't know.

"What colour are his eyes...and hair?"

Mrs Dunlop was unimpressed with my ignorance. "Aren't you interested in your brother? I'm sure you'll know how long he was when he came out of your Mummy's tummy."

I couldn't answer this question either. I wanted to tell Mrs Dunlop, I couldn't care less how long my brother was at birth and what he weighed. All I knew was his eyes were a different color to mine and that was that.

"I hope you will be a good helper to your Mummy, Mary!" said Mrs Dunlop as I returned to my desk.

In Primary three I never dared kick over the traces as I had in Primary two with Margaret Kyle. Mrs Dunlop was too terrifying. She belted me at times because I didn't do my sums properly. I never understood multiplication, particularly the seven, eight and nine times tables, but we learned the easy peasy eleven and very hard twelve times tables too. Mrs Dunlop dinned into us weights and measures: ounces, pounds, stones, feet, yards also.

Occasionally, I heard my parents giving a person directions, "It's two or three hundred yards!" I wondered how they could judge such a distance. Before the War, Dad trained as an architect and when he visited a house to plan an alteration or extension, he measured lengths by placing his feet one in front of the other, but he had to make allowances for his being unusually large.

With weights, fourteen was easy, being the number of pounds in a stone. Because tons and gallons were used for huge weights or volumes, I never understood their true value. Leagues, farthings and guineas were just for fairy tales. Only giants stepped in leagues, not humans. The wren, our tiniest bird, appeared on one side of a farthing. Guineas, amounting to one pound and a shilling were classy and grand.

Although I came to manage imperial measurements, I failed when turning units into tens: I began by adding the right-hand column of figures and 'carrying' the unit of ten to the next. In Primaries one and two, teachers allowed us to show our workings by jotting down in miniature what we'd 'carried' over. But Mrs Dunlop didn't allow us this luxury.

"No more crutches," she warned. "You're too old for them!" But try as I might, I had to use them.

It wasn't all sums in Primary three. We made food containers into fun. At break-time we drank a free bottle of milk, but I had difficulty drinking this tepid liquid through a straw. Coming from a dairy farm, I knew how smelly the milking process was, and I could only drink milk if it was disguised in tea, puddings or as butter and cheese. The school milk bottles were closed, not with silver foil, but with a cardboard cover, set in the rim of the neck, and Mrs Dunlop made us save them. We cut a circular hole in the centres and made woolen pom-poms, by winding black, red or blue wool around the hole and over the outside edge of two cards placed one on top of the other. When the center hole was filled, we lined up beside Mrs Dunlop's desk. With a pair of scissors she cut the wool. The last stage was to tie a piece of wool round the centre of the woolen threads and remove the card.

In Primary three we learned Scottish history. Dora approved. "Did they learn you about the Bruce?" she asked as she turned over the toast beneath the grill.

"The man with the spider?" I asked.

"Aye!" Without yon spider, you wouldny hae the Bruce!"

The Bruce hid in a cave. A spider spinning its web there inspired him not to give up. For an afternoon out, Mum drove us to Glen Trool, a local spot, where we climbed a hill to a memorial that explained the victory of Bruce's men over the English.

"Clever, wasn't it? They were on the top of the hill waiting for the enemy below and, when they appeared, Bruce and his men

rolled boulders on to them! That's how they won the battle!"
Mum explained. I wondered how the English could have been so
stupid as to have allowed themselves to be at the bottom of a hill
when they knew the locals weren't at all friendly.

We had a lot to learn about Scottish history. My family and
everyone here were part of it.

It's still happening, but my parents didn't talk news.

We had no appreciable enemy though, apart from my teacher, Mrs Dunlop. As farm children, however, we faced many dangers but Mum, and more so Dad, were largely unconcerned. Janet and Lis often popped out of their bedroom window, clinging to the outside of the sash and with their left foot, stepped on to the lead connecting the front section of the roof with the back. From there, they clambered to the top of the roof. When Dad discovered them, he complained, "Don't go on the roof again. It costs one pound ten shillings to replace each slate."

We had no central heating; only log fires in the sitting rooms, a stove fed with coal in the dining room and upstairs, electric bar heaters. If Dad saw we had switched ours on and positioned it close to our beds or a chair, he told us to be careful. "Don't burn the house down; we're not properly insured." A similar warning applied when he saw us crawling through the tunnel to the loft, "Watch out for loose wiring; you don't want to cause a fuse."

When it came to outside, he banned us from the hayshed where we burrowed into its centre through gaps in the bales. "If you tug the twine, it breaks; then the bale is ruined and each one costs a pound." Another danger was the midden. After milking-time, when the cows were in their stalls or out in the field, Bob Young mucked out the byre, shovelled the dung into his wheel-barrow and pushed it to the midden where he wheeled it along a plank lying on top of the heap, to empty the contents at the far side. When no grownup was looking, we dared each other to walk the plank, like pirates.

I liked Long John Silver from "Treasure Island' as I was used to real people with a missing limb. Uncle Jock lost his leg in France when he stepped on a booby trap in the war, and I was friends with a girl whose Dad managed the Newton Stewart branch of the British Linen Bank. He also had a limp but I never knew why. Long John Silver was much more interesting than my uncle or the bank manager; he was a villain and, as Mum said, the devil often has the best tunes. The pirate may have been a cripple but he was strong and had a laugh like ten thousand marbles spilling down a cantilever staircase, or of waves crashing across a pebble beach. I practised Long John Silver's walk in my bedroom. I even strapped Dad's walking stick to my right leg to feel what it was like to be unable to bend my leg. Then I mimicked Long John's laugh. From my diaphragm I gave a great roar, letting the sound fill the room.

We loved to touch and smell dogs' noses, cats' claws and horses' manes and fall into grass, hay, grain and mud. It was fun too to imagine the midden as the rough sea, its rivulets of rotting manure, a wall of waves and spume. One day I had the idea of blind-folding Lis and making her walk the plank. "I can't!" she was terrified. "I won't see where to put my feet and, if I fall off, I'll sink right up to..." Lis couldn't finish her sentence.

"Come on!" I tried to encourage her. "OK, I'll make you a bargain. If you go first, I'll follow!"

Lis shook her head. "You go. You're the eldest."

I had no way around her argument. I had to go. I knew also that if I misjudged my step, I'd fall off the plank into the dung and might sink as far as my neck or even worse. Lis grabbed the scarf from Janet, covered my eyes with it, tying its ends at the back of my head.

"There!" she said. "Go!" She pushed me towards the edge of the plank. It was now my turn to be frightened. I wasn't good at balancing. I was bad. I could just about hop along the garden path outside the greenhouse but I couldn't do handstands, far less a cart-wheel. As I felt my way in my wellingtons, arms outstretched for balance, my heart beat hard.

"What's it like," I heard Lis ask, "to drown in cow dung?"

"Filthy!" was Janet's reply.

"Horrible!" Lis added and I trembled at the thought of my neck going under, then the dung reaching my mouth, nose and finally my eyes. "No, no, no!" I gasped. "I can't." I tugged at the scarf, untied it at the back, and let it fall into the manure. It lay there for a moment before it sank.

We had plenty of dangerous places on the farm. Apart from

the midden, there was the Moss where a sea of liquid peat, the colour of dark chocolate, surrounded islands of bracken, myrtle and heather. The Moss covered acres of ground and, according to Dad, was like much of the land in Wigtownshire in the old days before it was drained. "Impossibly impassable!" he said. "If you weren't careful, you could step into that peat and sink right up to your middle. You didn't need Sawney Bean; the Moss was as frightening as any cannibal."

One breakfast-time, after Dad had finished eating his bacon and eggs and Mum had drunk her second cup of coffee, he said strangely, "I'm getting rid of it!"

"You should!" Mum answered.

"I don't want to get caught."

"What would happen if they discovered you still had it?"

"Dunno!" Dad shook his head. "I'd get a warning or a fine. Maybe, heaven forbid, a jail sentence. Who knows?"

"You'd better do it now."

Only later did I know what Dad had to do. He and Mum hid the nasty side of life. "Not in front of the children," she advised. They managed to conceal most unpleasantries of country life; for Sunday dinner Mum roasted a chicken and would ask Dad to first carry it away from the house up to the end of the field where we wouldn't see him wringing its neck.

This time, the secrecy hid Dad's having missed another amnesty for handing in firearms issued to servicemen in the war. In his case, it was a revolver. Dad decided to bury it on the Moss. I can imagine him doing it. I'm sure he chose a particularly deep spot. With its soup of gurgling peat, it was a perfect place to get rid of the firearm.

And there was the Cree, lying like a fat snake at the end of the field next to the double Dutch barn. When we first arrived, Mum and Dad warned us: we mustn't visit the river. It was the only time when they insisted on our safety. Don't go there, they repeated. Much like the evils of the midden, the Cree was dangerous. If we trod on the mud we would sink without trace, they said, but we learned later that it's not quick sands that kill. You sink into them but not that far. You're more likely to drown under the incoming tide. The river rose up in the hills but by the time it reached Carsenestock, it was wide, its bank sandy in places, muddy in others. Next to the sand and mud were 'the inks' or saltings: huge rectangles of grass like football pitches that flooded at high tide. Sea pinks grew there, and mushrooms interrupted the grass in September.

Bob Young went there with sacks to pick and sell the mushrooms in Newton Stewart. He could do that as the inks were not Dad's property. They belonged to the Crown. The cows went out on the inks in summer and fed off its rich grass. During an unusually hot spell, when they wished to cool themselves, half a dozen tested the waters of the Cree and got stuck in the mud.

Bob discovered the cows in the river then and cried for help. Dad rushed to the inks with Tony on the wee grey Fergie and extended a ladder across the mud until it reached the nearest cow.

She was young and panicky. While Bob tried to calm her, Dad slung a rope around her neck, attaching the other end to the front of the tractor. Tony shoved its gear into reverse and gently applied his foot to the accelerator. It didn't work. The cow hurled its head from right to left and the rope broke. They repeated the exercise but the rope broke again. "There's nothing for it but to wait till the tide comes in, and pray," said Dad. Bob returned to the byre to milk the rest of the herd, while Dad waited with Tony by the river.

Mum arrived with tea and sympathy for the cows, at least. Seeing the distress of the beast nearest to the bank, Mum rushed to help. "I'll calm this one down!" She grasped the end of the ladder and crawled towards the cow. "There, there," she said, trying to console the creature. She looked into the whites of the cow's eyes and saw its anguish. "You'll be fine," she said. "Dinny fash!" But when she saw its tongue hanging from its mouth, she panicked. "This cow needs water, David! We must get it for her. Now!"

By the river there was none, except salt water.

"Someone fetch a bucket of fresh water," she insisted, casting a glance at the other captives. "It looks as if they all need some."

"We won't be able to reach the others," Dad protested.

"I'll have a bloody good try!"

"I forbid you to. It's too dangerous! We don't want you getting drowned."

"Nonsense! I won't drown!" The drama grew serious. It was one thing to lose cows to quick sands or the tide, but another to watch your Mum swallowed by the waves. That's what had happened to the Wigtown Martyrs. Not far downriver, two Covenanting women were tied to a stake and left to drown.

Tony appeared on the brow of the hill, carrying large buckets of water. Mum seized one and lugged it towards the ladder. In the end she only managed to reach three cows, those trapped closest to the grass. They were so thirsty, they drank all our fresh water. "Go home now, Esther!" Dad ordered. "We'll deal with them." But Mum remained on the inks until the tide came in and with the rush of water, each cow freed herself from the loosened mud and clambered on to the bank to safety.

THE COWS WERE our livelihood so they came first: so did the creamery truck that thundered down the farm road collecting the milk; the vet who climbed from his big car; the salesmen flogging detergents for the dairy and boiler house, and ointments for teat sores, and aluminum milk containers; even the knacker's lorry that collected fallen stock. Amongst these goings-on we played, not peevers anymore, as I had done with Margaret; nor tig with Lis, Janet, Anne and Gladys Young; not even flying on corn sheaves in the hayshed. We were ready for a new activity.

I liked gardens, not Mum's, arranged to look wild, when clearly it wasn't. Nor Bob Young's with rows of carrots, parsley, potatoes and onions. I wasn't that interested either in the space by the old cheese loft where Mum got us to sow nasturtium, cornflower and marigold seeds. "Don't dig them up!" she warned, when the day after we sowed them I wanted to see if the seeds had germinated.

In class, Mrs Dunlop taught us about cultivation. Holding out a piece of moist blotting paper, she spilled mustard seeds over it. Her idea was to combine botany with theology. "The Kingdom of Heaven is like a grain of mustard seed," she announced. " Her eyes scanned the entire class as she intoned the sources of her quote. "Matthew, chapter 13, verses 31 to 32, Mark, chapter 4, verses 30 to...." With her outstretched palm, she showed us a mustard seed. Jock Wallace flung himself over the desk we shared, straining to see what was in her hand, "...which a man took and sowed in his field, which indeed is smaller than all seeds. But when it is grown, it is greater than the herbs, and becomes a tree, so that the birds of the air come and lodge in its branches."

"Where does she get her ideas from?" I asked.

"She's reading from the bible. Can't you see? It's on her desk on top of the belt," Billy said.

The penny then dropped. Bibles and belts went together like horses and carriages. Whenever she belted us, she quoted Proverbs —chapter 13, verse 24: "Spare the rod and spoil the child."

The Bible was still confusing. On the one hand, it encouraged the small to grow big and strong, as acorns become oaks, but equally important was the idea of a big person cutting a small one down to tiny size by hitting.

One day when we were at the road-end waiting for the school bus, the thought came to me of creating our own garden, but not one with a brick wall and roses growing up it, like Mary Lennox's in 'The Secret Garden'. Ours would be special, bound by the Moss on one side, the road on the other, and six rowans at the far end, a space I could pin my dreams on. I lived by dreaming. Not the ones I had while asleep but those that swarmed in me during the day. Dora told me that dreams came from the land: from hills and glens that had been trodden on for generations. Not from asphalt or concrete, but the soil whether it was sand, peat, clay, rock or loam. "That's why yon Pope kisses the ground when he visits a country," said Dora. "The ground we stand and live on is the stuff of dreams. Not drams, mind!" she laughed. "Plenty live for them. If you stick your head in a dram, that's all you get, but dreams take you wherever you wish. Drink or drams or whatever you call them, destroy you, but dreams are the making of a man. Nobody lives without them."

I dreamed through my bedroom window at the hill. Though a grand lady had lived on it in her big house, and a German had met his death there, the hill was mine. It belonged to me, and I belonged to it. I pinned my hopes on it but knew I'd never possess it. I doubted if anyone could properly own anything. Who could dictate the laws of trespass, when birds, fish, beasts and bugs had no idea of ownership, except in their nests?

After we caught the bus and found our seats, I asked Lis if she liked my idea of making a garden beside the road. It wasn't only that I wanted to create it with her. I hoped to be her closest friend, to whisk her away from Janet and the Youngs. The garden would be ours and nobody else's. Lis turned and looked out of the window. She was never as keen as I to do things with me. I wondered what put her off. Friendship never came easily, but she nodded and I took it that she wanted to. We could plant all sorts of flowers, the bigger and blowzier the better. I liked the ones a mile up the road at Lamachan View, where people grew dahlias, gladioli, chrysanthemums, all blooms Mum disliked, but Lis and I wanted. Never mind that our soil was unsuitable. Virtually a swamp, it only let rushes, bramble and myrtle thrive. My garden fantasy, however, refused to evaporate and I conjured up images of roses with velvety petals, sweet-scented freesias, and narcissi with scarlet trumpets. Instead of planning where to plant our flowers and shrubs, Lis and I, on our first visit, pegged out a section of ground for a toilet and on returning home, stole from the back cupboard a roll of tissue to hook onto the branch of a birch tree. Our ground wasn't to be cultivated with smart plants like calendula or lobelia, but it was ours nonetheless: with secret paths encircling birch and gorse. It was the paths we dreamed of, that meandered around tussocks, dipped into hollows, and skirted peat sores that oozed water the color of stewed tea. In my wellingtons, I'd pick my way around them until I reached the fence with the Moss acreage beyond. The days we shared secrets were the best, better than when we went to the beach or stopped in Wigtown at de Prato's for an ice cream.

We knew each bank, clump, bog and quagmire as only native country children could. Like a rabbit whose nostrils dilate at any suspicion of danger, we sensed where not to tread, and when we had our first visitor, I forgot to guide her around Hellhole, the deepest bog in the garden. It gurgled and bubbled and threatened to suck us in if we dared try to cross it, but revealed its treachery by growing a beard of lighter coloured grass than the neighbouring vegetation, which was dark.

Through the garden, Lis and I forged a better relationship than before but at home I still felt rejected. Happy in their favoured pos-ition with Dad, my sisters continued to enjoy at bed-time his Johnny and Tommy stories. Dad introduced more extravagant exploits for these boys, involving eating and speeding in boats, planes or cars. Although they were aimed at children, the stories were biased towards Dad's open love of his excesses.

Not long after the departure of the Kyles, I made a new friend in Melanie Fraser. For me, she was a turn up for the books. She lived at Lamachan View in the house next to frightening Sheila Black whose front room curtains twitched whenever we passed. Melanie's mother was kind; her father was a Geography teacher at the Douglas Ewart, 'the big school' in Newton Stewart. We became friends because we lived close to each other and were in the same class, both of us sitting fairly high on the scholarly ladder. Each Thursday after school Melanie accompanied us on the bus and stayed for tea. One afternoon, Lis and I decided to show her our garden. When the bus stopped at our road-end, we clutched our schoolbags to our chests, jumped on to the asphalt and ran across the road to the garden entrance. Lis pushed in front of us and leapt over the stile. "See you later at the rushes by the myrtle wood," she shouted: we bigged up everything in our space.

As I placed my foot on the stile's bottom rung, Melanie in her elephant-brown gabardine, clutched my sleeve. "I'm not going in there with my shoes on!" They were the kind Lis and I would never wear, not even for church. They had heels, one and a half inches high, and a thin band running across the bridge of her foot and buttoning at the side.

For some time, I had tried to persuade Melanie to visit our garden. She liked the idea, but not the reality. It meant mud, thorns, cuckoo spit, bird mess, wind and rain. I slung both legs over the stile, treating the top bar like the horse we vaulted in gym. Melanie froze. She pursed her lips. She was thinking hard. Because I wanted her to share the garden, I had coaxed her into coming. I thought of climbing back to her side and offering her a piggy-back but she was too heavy.

"Take your shoes off and I'll carry them!" I suggested.

Her face turned as pink as the areas on old maps that marked the territory of the British Empire.

"I can't!" she wailed. Her foot fell back on to the ground. "My socks'll get wet…"

I couldn't understand why Melanie was unable to negotiate a simple obstacle like a stile. I wouldn't have hesitated to tear off my socks and shoes to scale a wall, climb a tree, or cross the Moss. But Mum wasn't Mrs Fraser, nor was Mr Fraser our father; our families were different; they didn't socialize much together. Melanie crouched towards the ground, the hem of her gaberdine touching the damp grass. Seeing her coat getting wet, she stood up, shook her head, framed with short curls, and said, "I'll keep my shoes on."

Placing her left hand on the top bar of the stile, she lifted her right foot to the lowest step, but courage failed her. "I can't do it!" I climbed to the top of the stile and held out my arm to help her over. She moved her pudgy frame towards the first step, then the second, until she reached the top. At that moment, a rustling came from the bushes ahead; it could have been a deer or a hare, but it gave Melanie a start. She would have fallen on to the ground, had I not gripped her right arm. "Jump, Melanie!" I urged. "Jump!"

"No, I canny!"

Closing her eyes, she clasped my hand, and leapt into the air away from the stile. Her left ankle caught on the lower step. She fell. "Are you alright?" I was worried.

Drawing her unhurt leg away from the fence, she flinched as she tried to stretch her injured one. "I've hurt myself!" she sobbed. I begged her not to cry and told her she would have to stand up and follow me. Knowing there was nothing else for it, Melanie raised herself from the ground and limped down the track behind me. Our progress was slow, "I want to go home," Melanie said. "I want my Mum!" she moaned. I ignored her protests and turned a corner by the bog myrtle, avoiding tussocks of rush until we found Lis lying on the heather, her arms outstretched.

"What took you so long?"

"Nothing!" I said defensively. I wanted to protect my friend. After all, Melanie was more mine than Lis'. By sharing a desk at school, Melanie and I were close. I helped her spell words, like 'difficult' and 'janitor'. In her turn, she gave me the answers to sums set by Mrs Dunlop, so I could avoid using 'crutches'.

Lis sat up, smoothed down her skirt and scraped with a stick, the mud from the soles of her shoes.

"Here!" she said with a wicked smile. "Let's go to the rowan and cast a spell?" She stood up and was away, skimming hillocks and bends as if she were a hare. Keeping up with my sister, I sped along behind her, throwing my friend a backward glance.

"Keep up, Mel!" I yelled. When Lis and I arrived at the turning where the right led to Hellhole and the left to the rowan, we now realized we'd lost Melanie.

"Where is she?" I was in a panic. "I thought she was following us! It's all your fault." I said. Through my stupidity, I'd lost Margaret and now it looked as if Melanie had deserted me too. In my anxiety I blamed Lis. "Right from the start, you were showing off, letting us see how fast you could run, when you know how slow Melanie is."

"How was I to know she'd fall and hurt herself?"

"You should be more considerate," I complained, asserting my seniority.

"Stop blaming me." Lis was angry. "If it makes you feel better, I'll go and find her. We'll meet at the rowan. OK?"

With Lis gone, I made my way to our tree. She was away a long time. All I could do was sit down, my head against the rowan's trunk, and wait. I'd been told all about its magical properties. If treated well, it wouldn't let you down, but if you tore a branch from a tree, its berries would drop and bring bad luck.

Dora knew all about the rowan: "I mind when farmers pin rowan sprigs over doorways to the byre. On the hill they herd the sheep through hoops of rowan branches."

"Why?" I had asked.

"To ward off the evil eye," she explained. "The rowan's a goddess of the hills. You dinny mess with it. Dinny pick its berries. It brings awfy bad luck. I mind how my mother lost a' her tatties after stealing from the rowans!"

Mum had said Dora was talking nonsense. To prove her point, she picked rowan berries to make jelly, which went well with venison and mutton but tasted too bitter to us. For Lis and me, the rowan was the center of our garden and served as an altar to our deity, more easily approached than the God we worshipped in church. Ours thrived in inhospitable places. A mountain ash, the rowan grew on rocks, clung to the sides of hills, spreading its roots through stone and scree. We refused to kneel, pray or sing hymns to it, but in August, when the berries ripened, we picked and crushed them to make juice, which we poured into the palms of our hands, pledging our loyalty.

The sun was beginning to set. Where were they?

"Yoo-hoo!" I heard a call from the birches. "It's us!" I recognised Lis' voice before the bedraggled pair appeared. Both were covered with mud well above the knee. Twigs were caught in their skirts and hair. Then I saw that Melanie's left shoe was missing. Pointing to her foot, I asked where it was.

Before my friend could reply, Lis regaled us with tales of what might have happened had she not been there to help. "You would have sunk without trace and got sucked in completely and have lain there for years, like those bog-people you see in museums and no-one knows how old they are. They could be one thousand years old."

I should have sided with Melanie and showed concern. Instead I joined Lis in her taunts, like an animal whose pack takes priority. "Someone will find your shoe a thousand years from now and ask what kind of person wore it." I said, giving Lis a furtive look. Melanie remained silent. In the soft evening light, her upper lip puckered and a tear rolled down her cheek. I had a terrible need then to put it all right. I felt guilty, unlike Lis, for it was our fault Melanie had lost her shoe.

Lis saw the adder first. "Look!" she said. "A big worm!"

Writhing on the peaty soil not more than four feet from where we stood, was a young adder. A sharp burst of sunshine had woken it from its sleep. None of us had ever seen a live snake before. "Stay away from it!" I gasped. "It might bite you!"

Melanie turned her face away and Lis shuddered.

I wanted to tell Mum. I knew she'd be cautious about trying to kill it, advising that snakes, like all living things, had a right to be. Everything in nature has its place, she often said. Even snakes and creepy crawlies, but I was too scared to wait for advice.

Being two years older than Lis, I seized control, pushing her and Melanie down the path towards the stile, away from the adder.

Running as fast as we could, I heard Lis say, "We'll tell Daddy. He can deal with it!"

He couldn't. All adults, even Dad, were banned from our garden. After Melanie sprained her leg and lost her shoe though, our enthusiasm for the garden weakened, and Melanie no longer wished to hear about my dream of growing phlox, honeysuckle, dahlia and gladioli in a squelchy bog.

She found another friend, who introduced her to intelligent board games, like Scrabble and chess.

Lis and I still visited our rowan tree, but our dreams of having a special garden soon ended.

Carsenestock with my hill beyond

"ISN'T THIS FUN?" Dad pulled up on the grass, opened the car door and climbed out. "Do you know who said that?" he yelled, to be heard above the wind. A blast of cold air hit my face as I stepped from the car. I slammed my door shut. "You've told us a million times!" I said, tired of Dad's forced jollity and his demand that we hide our feelings. "It was my dear mother, whenever we went for a picnic," he said, opening the boot to bring out a box of food. He chivvied the rest of us out of the car. "Come on, Lizzie. Hurry up, Janet. And you, Esther, no complaints. Isn't this fun?" he said again.

There'd been a row over where we'd go that day. Dad wanted to visit Kailzinet where he grew up, but Mum vetoed it. So did we. "The house is too big," Lis complained. "We can never find the bathroom there."

"It's dead poky!" said Janet, meaning scary. She had picked up the term at school, but it was true. We lived in a normal-sized house, Kailzinet was a barn of a place. Outside it was nice with pink sandstone walls and fairy-tale turrets, but on the way to the beach we saw a different house with windows of diamond-shaped panes, a blue door, a small but fabulous garden with a wishing-well and gnomes fishing on the bank of a pretend pond. Marigolds, phlox, sweet Williams and hollyhocks nodded together next to a cobbled path bordered with scallop shells. We drove past at a snail's pace to read the notice on the gate. 'Home sweet Home'.

"More like 'Gnome sweet gnome!' Mum laughed.

"For my money, when it comes to design," corrected Dad, "I like 'Rome sweet Rome.'" Trained as an architect, Dad felt he had the last word. Mostly he loved classical buildings with Doric, Ionic or Corinthian columns. Modern architecture with its fondness for flat roofs wasn't his choice.

"Now, Lizzie," he said, "you carry the rugs, Colin, the bottles and Janet, the cake tin. Dad handed her a container of chocolate biscuits and fairy cakes. Mum rummaged in the car's glove pocket for her field glasses. "Mustn't forget those, Mummy, must we?"

Dad reminded her. "As if I would!" she snapped, annoyed with him for calling her 'Mummy'. She always brought her binoculars; whether to a wood, a hill-side, the beach or a river, where she'd notice some bird or other and remark, 'That's not a common thrush, is it? It must be a waxwing. Why is it here at this time of year? Was it blown off course?" She couldn't say.

Maybe Mum's sister-in-law, Anne, who knew about birds, gardens and country things, might know.

"Follow me, everyone!" Dad loved organising us, even Mum who became indignant. She wasn't his child.

Much like our seat in church, we had a special place at the beach. It was on the first ledge of rocks before the cliffs rose up sheer. To reach it, we picked our way through the marram grass growing in the sand, taking care not to cut our legs or fingers on it. On our way, we passed deep hollows in the sand dunes where 'courting couples' lay. Hurrying past them, Dad distracted us by pointing out to sea at an object like a yacht or dinghy.

"They're not courting," said Lis after I referred to a couple in that way. "They're stuck to each other like limpits, kissing and..." She didn't say what else.

"Here we are!" Dad placed the box of groceries and bottles of juice on a rock. "Isn't this fun?" he repeated. "This box isn't a cast-off from Alec Drem's grocery round..." I could tell Dad was rev-ving up, not for a 'Johnny and Tommy' story, but for another of his imaginaries, "...but a lovely wicker basket of delicacies from Fortnum's, no less with, not your common or garden sardine paste; excuse me, Esther, why do we put up with that?" He picked up a jar of dark brown substance and threw it behind him on the sand. "Let it be magicked into the choicest anchovy paste, Gentleman's Relish, no less and this hideous meat paste is paté de foie gras and I don't feel the least bit sorry for those geese," he laughed.

When he'd emptied the box of delicacies, of diluted Kia-ora orange squash, jam sandwiches, crisps, a flask of milky coffee for Mum and Dad, a packet of digestive biscuits and a few oranges with wrinkled skins, we sat in a semi-circle like sheep sheltering behind a dry-stone dyke, backs to the wind, trying to keep warm and not letting sand cover our sandwiches. "It's all dirty!" wailed Colin. Mum pulled him on to her lap and removing the sandwich from his hand, wiped it, saying soothingly, "Here it is; eat up now!" Colin yanked it from Mum's hand and she watched him nibble fastidiously the corner of the salmon paste sandwich.

"Smugglers brought their contraband here!" Dad told us.

"Their what?"

"Contra-band means goods like brandy, wine and silk that they avoided paying tax on," he explained. "So they hid it from the excise officers whose job it was to collect money owed on these things. Robert Burns was an excise man in Dumfries; he hated the job and composed a poem about it."

Dad began to sing the words in a strong Dumfriesshire accent:

> The Deil's awa, the Deil's awa
> The Deil's awa wi' th' Exciseman.
> He's danced awa, he's danced awa
> He's danced awa wi' the Exciseman.

Robert Burns, the ploughman poet, was Dad's Number One hero; whenever he recited or sang his words, he did it with incredible seriousness, as if they were verses from the bible. His great, great grandfather had corresponded with Robert Burns, and Dad was especially proud of this.

On finishing the song, Dad looked up at the cliff. "Anyone want to climb with me?" he asked. "There's a path to our right and it's not too steep." Lis and I agreed to go, and Mum would follow with Janet and Colin. I saw her from time to time peering through her binoculars at fulmars and oyster catchers.

The sun made the water light up with a fluorescent twinkle and on the sea's surface, lighter than the rest of the water, was a gigantic patch reflecting the clouds in the sky. I watched the gulls flying between the two elements and wondered how deep the sea was and what lived in it. The plants of the sea were a mystery. Was it as deep as a mountain is high?

Lichen spotted the cliffs. When we reached the top we saw sea pinks in candy colours. Near us a wagtail strutted. Stone dykes, like land waves, followed the hill's contours. Hawthorn blossom and whin bushes reminded me of French knots in an embroidery. The tide swelled, and the rhythm altered from leisurely breves to hurrying quavers as waves slammed into the rocks. I never understood how some people disliked the sea. "It's all the same! Just a barrier, that's all!" they'd complain. I never tired of listening to the sea's heartbeat.

'Our day at the beach', is what Mrs Dunlop, still my teacher, got us to write. "Sharpen your pencils!" she ordered. Our teacher wasn't keen on letting us use pens, with nibs dipped into ink wells. She was worried that Eddy McIntyre, the blacksmith's son at Challoch, would treat his pen as a weapon. Anything with a sharp point was fair game for him. He had seen his father hammering out hundreds of sharp objects in his forge and this gave Eddy the idea that his pen was also a spear. According to Mrs Dunlop, it was better to be safe than sorry with Eddy. So, we were to write in pencil about our day at the beach, and if the lead got blunt, we sharpened our 'implement', or pencil, with her sharpener, the contraption fastened to the side of her table.

The title of my composition was simply 'At the Beach'. Mum called it an essay but I saw it as a story. I liked the idea of writing ever since Melanie told me she owned a five year diary with a gold lock. When I went to her house she showed me the key and where she kept it, in an envelope, which she hid under the carpet by the window.

"Why do you do that?" I asked.

"So that Mum doesn't read it."

"Why would she?"

"You don't know my Mum. She wants to know everything."

"My Mum's not like that," I told her. "She never looks at what I write. Mind you, Granny's different. When she comes to stay she's always poking her nose into our business. Anyway, I don't have a diary."

"You should!"

"I'd never keep it going. I'd do January, and by the middle of the next month, I'd give up!"

Whenever I began a story, I gave up quickly, as I never believed in what I wrote. Descriptions sounded silly on a second reading. When all was said and done, what was there to say? Wasn't it a little strange to start my composition about my day at the beach with Dad's refrain, 'Isn't this fun?'

Really, I wanted to write about things that Mrs Dunlop did not approve of, like the courting couples in the sand dunes. She'd have circled any reference to them with a red pencil and scribbled 'n/a', meaning 'not appropriate' in the margin. We learned quickly that in the classroom, some subjects were not to be mentioned, like loving couples and money.

I had another doubt, and that was the way Dad pretended our picnic came from Fortnum and Mason. Although Mrs Dunlop maybe knew Fraser's in Glasgow and Jenner's in Edinburgh, would she have heard of Fortnum and Mason in London and accuse me of being a snob? She might say, "What's wrong with Mr Drem, the grocer in Newton Stewart? If he's good enough for Dr Brown, for Mr Reid, the bank manager of the Clydedale, and for the Reverend Macdonald of St. John's Church, why shouldn't he be good enough for your family?"

At the picnic, after coming off the cliff, I ran as fast as I could along the shore till I saw a large shiny brown stone on the sand. I leapt on it and felt my feet sinking into a soft, yielding substance. I was standing on a jelly fish. "It's dead," Mum said, "or it might have stung you." So, sea creatures stung too. This was a first, but I'd been deceived before, like when Margaret Kyle stole my purse. I didn't believe it was her but Mum said it was. Mum let me take it to school, asking me to take special care as the purse had been hers when she was a girl. It held six or seven unpolished stones, from Iona, an island off the coast of Argyll. In a scuffle at the school gate, I dropped Mum's purse. I found the stones but her purse disappeared. The jelly fish was a sensation and a shock more than a deception. Could I explain my surprise to my teacher?

Though we lived near the sea, because of Dad the air was more our element, and the land. Ever since I knew him he was grounded though he had flown every imaginable aircraft from Bristols,

Gypsy Moths and even a Lancaster. I'd never seen him fly, so I once asked him the exact measurements of a Wellington bomber. Was it as big as a bus, a whale, or an elephant. "Very much bigger," he said. "Much, much?" I asked. He nodded. And then his eyes shuttered closed before me. Talking about war was a no-through road, a quick dead end to knowing him.

For my composition, I wrote just what was expected of me.

"My day at the beach was nice. I enjoyed it. We went in the car to Monreith. It was very windy and Dad said, as he always does when we go anywhere, isn't this fun? My Mum said nothing. She just kept looking through her bye-nokoolas." I knew Mrs Dunlop would underline that word in red and add 'Sp' in the margin, but I wanted her to. She'd already turned up her nose at the way I called the beach, the sea-shore. Other expressions I liked were as unpopular, like going 'up' to London or Oxford.

"What on earth do you mean, Mary?" she remarked. "Everyone knows that London's 'down' in England and not 'up' in Scotland." When it came to expressions for parts of the body, Mrs Dunlop asked if anyone called their oxter an armpit? I shot up my arm. "That's a very English way of naming that part of your anatomy," she sneered.

It was just as well that Mrs Dunlop didn't ask the class to write about our day at the beach again. At the start of the visit, Dad made his usual comment when we got out of the car and collected the rugs, a change of clothes and our picnic in a box from Mr Drem. We'd all sat down, Mum on the rug and me beside her, when I saw her normally calm, face crease, then crack. Her shoulders sank, like the collapse in the street of a Victorian carriage-horse. She thrust her left hand at Dad, who had just bit into a pork pie.

"Look! It's gone!"

"What's gone?"

"Can't you see?" Mum sobbed.

We leaned over her hand and stared at it. There they were, her gold wedding and engagement rings. The latter was one of a set. "Think of it, owning a set of diamond rings!" Melanie had gasped when I told her. "All my Mum's got is a wedding and eternity ring."

"What's an eternity ring?" I asked.

"A ring you have for ever," she replied. From the way Melanie smoothed her skirt with short, sharp pats over her knees and hesitated in answering my question, I realised she didn't really know.

"Anyway," I reassured her, "my Mum's only got one from that set. They sold the rest."

"Sold?" asked Melanie. "Why?"

To be honest, I didn't know. I never understood where so many things in our house went. One day when we returned from school, we saw that an old high-backed chair was missing, but I did learn that Dad had sold it to an Irish antique-dealer passing through.

I looked again at the row of diamonds on Mum's engagement ring and counted them: one, two, three but where was the fourth? "Look!" Mum wailed. "Can't you see?" There was a gap in the row, like the space in a row of teeth. Not one to be very concerned about precious stones, Dad stopped eating, shook his head and said, "Never mind!"

"Never mind?" Mum said. "I do mind. Is it properly insured?"

Dad shook his head. "You're right. It isn't, I'm afraid!" Paying insurance wasn't an option for him. As with everything else, Dad's shotgun, suits, not to mention his livestock, fodder and the fields themselves, were insufficiently insured. "We'll get an artificial stone," he suggested.

"Artificial? I ask you."

Dad's offer reminded Mum of her brother's artificial leg, which he acquired when his real one was amputated in the war. It reminded me of Dad's younger brother, Uncle Jim, who wore a denture for two absent teeth, knocked out in a game of football when he was eleven. Mum had a horror of the artificial, especially flowers and cream; even Bird's Eye custard. She always served trifles prepared with egg custard, perfected in a double saucepan, in spite of the risk of the mixture curdling.

"I won't have an artificial diamond, thank you very much!" she protested.

"What can we do? Get down on our hands and knees and search for it? Talk of a needle in a haystack!"

"Or a diamond in the sand!" I ventured.

"Shut up, Mary! I was going to leave the ring to you in my will!"

"No you won't!" Dad was firm. "It will go to Colin's wife! Daughters get your other jewellery but engagement rings go to the daughter-in-law, just like you got this ring from my mother."

"Who cares now that it's ruined!" Mum said.

She turned her back on us and gazed up at the sky. "At least I still have my field glasses, the only other present of worth that you have ever given me, David."

Monarch of the Glen - David S Gladstone
better known at home as Dad

WHEN IT CAME TO THE WAR, Dad buried the past much like he did when he sank his revolver into a peat bog on the Moss. Before he bought this farm, he visited one in Galloway with a herd of seventy cows. He could have made hay with hardly needing to cut a drain or add more than a bag of lime to the soil, but for the fact its fields lay close to a war-time aerodrome. After ambling across the runway, blistered with weeds and thistles and touring the crumbling buildings of prefabricated concrete with asbestos roofs, he passed on that farm. In the end, my Dad insisted on one with a view, not to his past but to the future, one with a horizon and skies he could paint rather than those he must invade or risk being shot from, even in memory.

Mum too wanted to forget. At the beginning of hostilities, she exchanged her mauve and green school uniform for khaki. She hated that colour and never dressed us in it; not even beige or pale brown. "It's supposed to be the color of dust, and a perfect camouflage, but it just reminds me of shit," she confessed. Sometimes she used military expressions learned while she was a young officer in the Auxiliary Territorial Service. Once, when she and Dad made an appointment with Mrs Dunlop to discuss my school progress, she advised me to stay at home with Dora because I was 'surplus to requirements.' Picking brambles, she told me that during the war, people let the berries rot on the bushes because they hadn't enough rationed sugar to make jelly or jam.

My parents wished those war years, like fading scars or words scrawled in the sand, washed away by the tide. If Mum and Dad were serious about forgetting, why, I began to wonder, did they hire German au pair girls to look after us? After the war, during the early years of their marriage, a generous supply of young German women wished to learn English. They were taught it in school and listened to the occupying American and British radio networks, but many preferred to learn the language in England, staying in homes like ours for at least one year before returning to Germany.

Mum spoke strongly about these young women, but I could

not remember any well, except Helga, the last one. When we moved north, Mum stopped hiring foreign au pairs and employed local women like Dora instead.

All were a substitute for proper nannies, who wore uniforms and played a vital family role. Our cousins loved theirs, who did not stay for a year or a Christmas, but for life. When the children grew up and had no more need for their nanny, the family provided a pension, kept in contact, and even visited her when she was old and living in a Home. Our au pair girls were different; they were young, inexperienced, troubled perhaps, and troubling. Barely able to cope with the war and what befell her brothers, Mum found them very difficult. "Except Trudi!" she admitted. "She was fun! I could always rely on her! She knew how to help, soothing you when you were teething, frying sausages for Dad's breakfast, and doing the ironing beautifully. I couldn't cope with Martha. She was a clever linguist. Every evening, she listened to the wireless, tuning to Radio Hamburg, Radio Paris, Prague, and even Moscow."

"Why?"

"She was convinced there would be another war, possibly between Russia and the West, and this time….."

"It'd be curtains?"

Mum nodded "…for us all. As for our Helga, she was Swiss, but impossible."

How could she have been? I loved the way she lifted me on to her lap and, rocking me backwards and forwards, sang 'Hoppe, hoppe Reiter', an old German song meaning 'Bumpety, bump, rider'. The song itself wasn't comforting; a man on horseback sets out on a long journey but falls into a pond and is lost without trace; he's tossed into a ditch and eaten by ravens, then lands with an almighty splash in a swamp, but Helga made me feel wonderfully happy. When she reached the final line, she'd open her legs and let me fall gently on to the floor. How could she be 'impossible'? I didn't want her to be in my past. What was more she had promised to write as soon as she got back home.

I waited each morning for the postman to arrive. I'd worked it out. At 9 am, the creamery lorry blundered down our road, ob-literating in autumn all the inkcaps and late daisies growing on the verge. The postman arrived half an hour later.

"Any letters from abroad?" I'd ask.

He'd shake his head. "No, lassy!" he said, riffling through the mail. "Jist two big brown envelopes, a wee bill from Mr Owen, the butcher, the newspaper from London and two boxes, I dinny ken what they are. Nuts and bolts for the dairy, maybe."

He dumped the letters and packages on the table by the back door, returned to his van, and drove off.

In the end, I gave up waiting, not knowing why Helga broke her promise. "I'll send you a card of an edelweiss," she had said.

"What's that?"

"A tiny, white flower that grows in the Alps. It's difficult to find because it is so rare. Many boys have died climbing rocks to pick one for their girl-friends."

I'd heard of knights on horses fighting duals to win the hand of a lady but never a Swiss boy risking his life to pick a flower.

Mum never told me why Helga was 'impossible'. I found out when Mum's friend, Elizabeth Campbell-Paisley, came to visit. E C-P, we called her, was the church organist and a keen rider who attended meetings at the pony club on Desmond, her bay gelding. "Did you know that Helga was sweet on David?" Mum explained while they drank coffee in the television room. "It was not just the way she moved her hips as she carried sausages in-to the dining room; she would flash him a silly smile with her Yardley's Burnt Orange lips! I ask you, Burnt Orange! But it was better than her Candy Floss."

I'd never seen Mum look so cross and was glad I'd hidden in an armchair behind the standard lamp.

"It was worst at breakfast-time. Her eyes followed him right around the room and stopped at the place where he ate. When he stood up and headed for the sideboard to fill his cup of coffee and collect the newspaper, there they were, studying his every move. I got tired of her eye-lashes, fluttering like the wings of a trapped butterfly. I'm sure she used what's called mascara to blacken them.

She had to go, though she was so good with Mary. It was sad."

One afternoon, Elizabeth invited us for tea at Birch Glen, where she lived with Mrs Smythe, her ancient mother in a big house. The first time we visited, she pushed us into the old lady's room on the ground floor and told us to line up according to our age and height. First me, then Lis, and finally Janet.

"Who is the eldest?" asked the old lady. After explaining who was who, we listened to Mrs Smythe's advice. "I hope you're good girls and not too much trouble to your mother!"

We assured her we were good.

"Are you old enough to go to parties?"

I'd be ten on my next birthday; our only social engagement was the school Christmas party and another at Sunday School.

"Not yet!" I volunteered.

"As soon as you're old enough, go to them. We don't want your mother worrying about you in her old age!"

Mum had read us a book about girls hanging out in a country house waiting for someone to marry them. Were we also expected to do this when we were older?

Apart from playing the church organ, E C-P wrote nativity plays for children who performed them in the village hall. Her best efforts were historical sketches for the annual pageant. She told us: "The old drover's road to Edinburgh runs past the back of our house! Drovers drove the cattle to market by foot. They forced cattle from the islands to swim to the mainland for their long journey to the cities."

The drovers gave Elizabeth an idea, to write a play about them on the old roads. She dreamed up hilarious scenes for 'The Drunk Drover': his beasts escaped, broke into villagers' gardens, and gobbled up the Minister's cabbages. They stole from hay-stacks and scoffed a straw hat belonging to the lady of the manor. E C-P steered us away from the drovers' real misdemeanours: cursing, fornication and filching from the towns they passed through. I could see the hardy cattle, reared on inhospitable ground like the Moss of Cree, traipsing their way across country in large herds.

For costumes, crinoline dresses and frock coats, Elizabeth roped in Mrs Boyce, the gardener's wife to make them. A fantastic seamstress, Mrs B was different from other Galloway men's wives. She spoke in a foreign accent; not French like our neighbour's wife, a glamorous Parisian, but in a more guttural way. On one visit, when she came out of her cottage with a basket of washing, Elizabeth nudged Mum in the ribs, "Pas devant les enfants!" she mumbled. "Mary mustn't find out what happened to poor Mrs B."

I wanted to ask why Elizabeth pitied her but didn't dare. She was determined to keep the secret. Had Mrs B been kidnapped, sent to jail, been suffering from an incurable disease or, against her will, forced into having a baby? It was odd. She looked happy enough and I liked Andy, her son, who rode on Jingle, Elizabeth's New Forest pony, with me on Marty, to pony club meetings.

One afternoon, as I followed Mum and Elizabeth to the field where Desmond and Jingle grazed, they told me that Mrs B was Jewish and before the war, she'd lived in Austria. When the leader of Germany, an evil man called Hitler, invaded, she escaped to Britain and found a job as a maid with Elizabeth's mother. I learned little else about Mrs B, except she was the only person in her family to survive the war. "What about the others?" I asked.

"Sent to concentration camps, to work and be starved to death, or gassed."

"What do you mean?"

"I don't want to go into it, Mary," said Mum. "They died, and after the war ended, Britain and America made the Germans who lived near the camps watch film footage of what they found when they liberated them. After watching it, many came out crying, claiming they had no idea what was going on down the road."

"A likely story!" Elizabeth interjected with sarcasm. "You know, Esther, I still don't understood why Churchill failed to use the murder of Jews as propaganda against Hitler."

"My happiest story about the war," said Mum, "was seeing a black G.I. march a platoon of German prisoners-of-war along a station platform. I wanted to go up and ask them where was their 'Deutschland, Deutschland, uber alles' now?"

Whenever I visited Elizabeth, I saw Mrs B either pegging out washing on the clothes' line or watering plants, specially her herbs that stood in pots on the window ledge of her kitchen. In summer when it was hot, she walked down to Desmond and Jingle's field, leaned on the gate and, to keep the flies off them, waved from side to side a leafy branch over their heads. "I seen dem; hundreds of bloody flies. Dee horses no sodding like dem."

In all the years she'd lived in Scotland, Mrs B only learned a smattering of English, but she picked up from her Galloway husband, plenty of swear words which she used freely. Elizabeth often wondered how the couple communicated other than with four letter words. Really, Mrs B reminded me of a swan transformed into an ugly duckling, her exotic plumage yielding to the rough culture and climate of her adopted country.

It took a visit to Monreith House for me to find out more.

The Wigtownshire mansion, surrounded by arable farms, stands in lush Scottish countryside. In the eighteenth century, its owner moved from a fortified house with crumbling ramparts to this Georgian pile whose sash windows let the weak Wigtownshire sunshine into its large rooms. For us, Monreith was a fading place of past grandeur, but Mum and Dad persuaded us to visit. Its owner, Aymer Maxwell, an aristocratic but failed film director did not live there any longer, having hived off to Euboea, a Greek island lying close to Athens.

"Why does he want to live so far off?" asked Dad. "He may avoid our horrible winters but Euboea isn't all that different."

"Don't be silly, David," Mum argued. "It's got sun, retsina, olives and lovely, long evenings to lounge outdoors in the heat. How often can we sun-bathe in the garden or swim in the sea?"

"I'll grant you, from what I've read, Euboea, like Wigtownshire, was a cradle of civilisation. The Greek alphabet was invented there, while Ninian, the first Christian missionary to Scotland, arrived near here. In the end both places became primitive. They fed the hungry cities of Greece and Scotland, of course. Euboea means 'the land of the well-fed oxen'. Just so. Who can deny that the best cattle in Scotland come from Wigtownshire?" Mum and Dad finally agreed on that.

This time, when we arrived at Monreith, Michael, Aymer's nephew was keeping house.

"Come in, Mawy!" crowed a large, young man standing at the front door. "Did you have a good dwive?" he asked. "It's a vewy twisty woad, isn't it?"

We entered a huge hall with dark portraits of Maxwells on the walls. Each brocade curtain was torn, and cobwebs hung like swags from the ceiling.

"Wight!" began Michael, who enjoyed ordering us around. "Lunch first, then hide and seek. We've plenty of hiding places."

As I took my place at a large mahogany dining table, I saw that the wallpaper pattern of ivy competed with the real McCoy.

"Isn't it dweadful!" said Michael, as he noticed me looking at a branch of green leaves snaking around a painting with a chipped gilt frame. "I've twied to get my uncle to patch up the walls, so the jungle only gwows outside the house. But he doesn't listen. He pwefers to hide on his Gweek island."

In spite of the cobwebs, we enjoyed our game. Outside, it was sunny; mallards swam on the pond, blackbirds sang in the over-grown garden, and we hid behind the chestnut trees and in a wood-shed by the wash-house.

Inside and upstairs, we found a four-poster to crawl under. A better hidey-hole was the airing cupboard by the master bed-room. It was me who first discovered the library, a roomful of books, smelling of decay, their pages curling. Damp had bent their covers and broken the spines but there they were, row upon row, testaments to the past when rich men fed their minds too, with a patrician diet of the classics: Aristotle, Epicurus, Cicero, Homer, Gibbon, Burke, Locke, Hume, Fielding, Swift, Scott, Pope, Byron, Shelley, Coleridge, and Browning for good measure. Polymath Sir Herbert, Michael's great-grandfather, had enlarged the collection, adding tomes on local history, topography, biology, horticulture, and Mum's favorite, ornithology.

I scanned the shelves, regretting that most of the authors were so long dead. Where was the present? There, sandwiched between 'The Interpretation of Dreams' and 'On the Origin of Species', it was, with its new cloth-bound cover, belying what was inside. I opened the book and turned to the first page where I saw an image of a man, or possibly a woman, wearing striped pyjamas. The face, with its large eyes was unaware of the camera. I turned the page again and found more starving figures, more striped pajamas and more skeletal faces. I'd heard the words, 'after Auschwitz, only silence.' I heard them again. The events of the mid-century took me by the scruff of my neck and shook me violently. This was Mrs. B's terrible concentration camp.

The door opened. "Mawy! Why are you here? Stop this bookworming! What are you weading? Put that away. It's a lovely day and we're going to play a game of cwoquet. Come and join us. You're not allowed to think here, still less dweam about anything else. You're here for fun, don't you understand? Fun, fun, fun! Just be happy and pwetty. Vewy pwetty. That's all you need be."

Cousin Nancy Rogers' wedding: Norman Macdonald Lockhart, Duncan James Maclean, Sue Macdonald Lockhart, Colin Gladstone, Jane Maclean, 1961

ON THE FIRST SUNDAY of each month, we had lunch with cousins. Following a lonely, hill road, we saw Clatteringshaws, a man-made loch with a huge dam that loomed over us as we drove past. It frightened Lis. Each time we approached, she hid her eyes from the vast concrete curve.

I was never relaxed at Kailzinet, now my uncle's house. Its hugeness made me feel tiny. "Look at all our windows," said my cousin when I stayed there on my own. We were sitting on the lawn close to the front door. "We have as many in one wall as you have in the whole of your house!" he said. I couldn't argue. It was obvious that Kailzinet was gigantic, almost as big as our double Dutch barn by the midden. My cousin's comment pointed out to me his higher class status. My house, Carsenestock, being bigger than Margaret Kyle's or Melanie's made me smug, but I had to admit that my cousin out-stripped me on those stakes.

Situated at the end of a winding drive, Kailzinet had woods, a walled kitchen garden, a farm and even its own 'far loch'. Dad envied his big brother, who inherited nearly all my grandfather's money. In our eyes still, one house was as good as another. Ours was warmer and, unlike our cousins, we got treats, like ice cream and comics on Saturdays, Mars bars from Willie Paterson's van, plus Mum allowed us children's television on Sundays.

A stuffed bear greeted us at the front door of Kailzinet. In its paw it held a pewter plate with calling cards from Reverend Lister, Mr Gilroy, Lady Paignton and Dr. McIlwraith, names that sounded like the characters from a game of Cluedo, from another age when visiting was formal and everything carefully noted, if not by the family, then by the servants. Details were not left to chance.If guests stayed overnight, they signed the Visitors' Book. Everything by the front door was old except two pairs of child's wellingtons; one, bright red, the other, sky blue, and an enormous pair of brown brogues, belonging to my uncle. At six foot seven, he was the tallest man I'd ever seen and made me feel even smaller.

The stairs leading to the drawing and dining rooms were as

broad as a race track and had shallow treads. Not like ours that were steep and narrow. These were wide enough to allow a lady or two in crinolines to climb or descend them together. I'd seen pictures of crinolines, under dresses with balloon-like skirts. When Dora left us, Pat, her replacement wore skirts like that, only hers were short with hemlines that reached just below the knee. She wore many petticoats to make her skirts stick out; I counted five. On her day off, she went out with Billy, her boyfriend, to Wigtown's De Prato's ice cream parlor, a focus for mods, rockers and teddy boys who came to hear Roy Orbison, Cliff Richard, Elvis, Helen Shapiro and Buddy Holly, "That'll be the day, aye-hey, That'll be the day!" on the juke box. Pat's special favorite was Bill Haley and the Comets. When we drove to town, Lis and Janet dared me to enter, which was risky. I might be mocked. A glance at my cords, round-toe lace-ups and gaberdine could make the winkle-picker girls with beehive hairdos crease up. I didn't go in. Luckily, Mr de Prato went the rounds of the farms. He came to us each Sunday, blasting his horn, the sound was his one-note jingle. He only sold one flavor: vanilla but it was deliciously creamy and came in a cornet or a wafer. If we were lucky, Mum bought us one nestling inside two nougat wafers, filled with a sweet, gooey cream and smothered in chocolate and coconut flakes. The oyster was a wonderful variation, a confectionery crustacean cupped in a nougat shell.

At Kailzinet, to the right of the wide staircase and lining the wall all the way up were glass cases, each with a different bird, anything from an auklet to a wren: birds from wood, estuary, moor, hillside, field, hedgerow and sea. Each was stuffed. The mind boggled at the challenges met so well by the taxidermist. I didn't ask how the birds came there, but Dad said his father was a keen shot. Shooting was his passion: grouse, pheasants, partridge, snipe, even wild duck and geese. At the dinner table he had a taste for game. When they removed his appendix, the surgeon discovered it contained a record number of shot gun pellets. This finding was then published in the medical journal, The Lancet.

Like Clatteringshaws dam, the birds in the cases frightened Lis.

"It's their horrible glassy eyes!" she whispered before hiding her own with her hands. Then she jumped up the stairs two at a time to escape quickly. Halfway up was a 'trompe l'oeil'.

"A tromp lay?" I asked.

"An optical illusion," Dad explained.

Nobody would have guessed the door into the gents' toilet. It looked just like the wall, covered with wallpaper. Kailzinet had another illusion too. At the foot of the garden was a ha-ha.

"Why call it that?" I asked.

"It wasn't funny for all those men who made it!" Dad replied. "But people in big houses liked wide views reaching as far as the eye could see, from garden to fields of grazing sheep. The last thing they wanted was a fence or hedge to interrupt. The answer was to build a sunken wall so the eye could travel into the distance unhindered. Isn't that a marvellous idea?"

"People went to ridiculous lengths to avoid reality!" said Mum.

"They still do! Take Hollywood block-busters!" Dad argued.

As we reached the top of the stairs, Aunt Louise darted out of a room on the left. "Good, you've arrived!" she exclaimed. "Lunch is ready. Children, go upstairs to the nursery! Esther and David, come in to the library and have a glass of sherry!"

We weren't eating in the dining room with the grownups then. I wasn't bothered, except I wanted to see the silver ship on the sideboard. The Gladstones had been ships' chandlers, Dad told me, that this miniature vessel served as the family insignia. As a pawnbroker is known by his three balls, a blacksmith by his anvil, and a carpenter by his adze, we had our ship. The Victorian period was a silver age for the family, so the ship's bow, stern, paper-thin sails, tackle, masts and ropes were cast in sterling silver, as if to say a Gladstone could wave his trader's wand and all he touched turned into silver.

I loved the precious sails, the delicate rolls of silver rope, and the pencil-thin masts but the ship was empty of passengers and crew. It sat gleaming on the dining room sideboard beneath the family portraits, like a miniature ghost ship. Upstairs at Kailzinet, I'd seen other family miniatures: dolls' houses modelled on the

Gladstones' original homes in Liverpool and London but people-less also, just as all Dad's paintings, hanging on our wall at home, were empty of any living creature.

With our cousins leading the way, Lis, Janet and I stumbled up a second flight of stairs, as wide and shallow as the first, passing on the windowsill an enormous bowl of dead petals, supposed to give out a sweet scent, but smelling musty instead. At the top of the stairs were the nursery and Nanny. She had a florid face, a sing-song voice, and wore dark blue overalls. Before we sat at the table, she made us visit the bathroom, but she wasn't frightening. She never asked us to say Grace before or after our meal, which was just as well as we knew none. Nobody, not even Mum, said it at home. Dad knew no Grace, or wasn't letting on that he did. Neither did the nanny get us to use table napkins. "Please don't call them serviettes!" Mum pleaded.

When I was baptised though, someone gave me a silver napkin ring in the shape of a swan and inscribed with the initials, MCG.

Another time, when Mum drove me to another house, not quite as large as my uncle's, I wasn't so lucky.

Along a corridor in a small room were two dozen green, blue, and white budgies but the nanny there didn't let me spend any time with them. "You can see them later, Mary!" she advised.

"In the meantime," she cleared her throat loudly, "I want you to meet Master Angus and Miss Catherine." A small, fair-haired girl, two years younger than me, gave me a curt nod of her head while her extremely tall brother, two years older, mumbled something that I didn't understand. I didn't know what to say, so I remained silent. I didn't like them or their nanny; Nanny Simpson or Simmy, as Angus called her, wasn't kind like my Kailzinet cousins' nanny.

"Simmy, what's for lunch!" asked Angus.

"Wait and see. It's a surprise!"

"Better not be a shock!" Angus smirked.

"Well," she began, "Catherine's having sugar 'n spice and all things nice and you, Master Angus, are having..."

"It'd better not be slugs, snails and dogs' tails!"

"Yuk! Imagine it," Catherine screwed up her nose in disgust.

Overwhelmed by my shyness, I said nothing but felt angry. Why weren't they nicer? After all, I was their guest. I wanted to complain to Mum but she was outside in the garden with Angus and Catherine's Mum, inspecting her flower border. They talked to each other all about plants. "How do I stop my camellia leaves turning yellow? Is it worth growing autumn crocuses on my lawn? How do you get your agapanthus to flower so well?

Nanny Simpson ordered us into a room next door to the budgie birds. "Sit down everyone!" The sideboard held a dish of stew. She dumped two spoonfuls and a boiled potato on a plate for me, three spoonfuls went on Catherine's plate, and four for Angus. It was a mystery why she gave them more food than I, but I picked up my fork and thrust it into a piece of meat.

"Not so fast, Miss! Don't you say Grace at home?"

My cheeks burned.

Nanny Simpson turned to her right. "Catherine, you're first!"

"For what we're about to receive," intoned the fair-haired girl, "may the Lord make us truly thankful."

Angus in Latin, followed: "Benedic nos domine et haec...tua largitate sumpsimus, per Christum dominum nostrum. Amen."

"Now, you, Mary!"

I bowed my head, placed the palms of my hands together, and mouthed silently, "God, help me to get away with this." Then I remembered hearing that if you wanted to sound as if you were talking on stage in a play, you murmured 'rhubarb, rhubarb...'

"What are you saying?" asked the Nanny. "Is it rhubarb?"

I nodded. "Are you thanking the Lord for the pudding you are about to receive? How did you know it was rhubarb crumble?"

I had a good mind to own up, to tell her, I hadn't the foggiest, that I was just pretending to say Grace, but I gave her a smile instead, hoping to satisfy, if not disarm her. It did the trick. But when the pudding arrived, something else I was expected to eat, that I couldn't stand, came with the rhubarb crumble. It was a nasty-looking grey mess that looked like frogs' spawn. I rebelled.

"No pudding?" Nanny queried.

I shook my head

"Well, you won't marry your French Count then, will you?"

This was beyond me. The woman saw I was puzzled. "If you don't eat up your food, you won't grow into a bonny lassy who attracts the boys, and, in your case, you'd be wanting a French count, at the least." She offered a smile but it wasn't warm. It had the hint of a sneer. I took up the spoon of congealed sago and tried to eat it. But I couldn't. I slammed it down so hard on the plate that bits of goo splattered on to the polished table. I stood up and ran out of the room. I didn't want tapioca, sago, nor a Nanny, neither a big, cold house with a spiteful Catherine or her gangling brother. Neither did I want a French count and, if it meant having to do that, what Lis and I had once discussed behind the boiler house at home, I certainly didn't want it either. Ughhhh. Think of that thing of his inside me.

Aunt Anne, Mum's sister-in-law, never frightened me. Granny and her cronies did. When they complained about the way I dried spoons or knitted a sock, I felt like Alice in Wonderland, as she disappeared down the rabbit-hole. I'd get a sinking feeling and down I'd go. I knew now how Alice felt when she changed size.

When I stayed at Granny's I felt very small. In spite of my height, by the time she had driven me to Campbeltown for church, I felt as tiny as a mouse, ready to dive for any rabbit-hole. How far would I fall? 5,000 miles? To the other side of the world? And if I reached it, would it be summer when here it was winter, or winter there if it was our summer? I wasn't sure.

Sometimes when I went up to my room, I pretended to be two Marys and would make up a conversation between myselves.

I'm unhappy.

Nonsense! You can't be!

Well, I am.

Pull yourself together! What have you to complain about?

Plenty, thank you very much.

The trouble was these conversations ended with me feeling worse than I did before, and I wasn't good at the ones where one Mary was nicer to the other.

Why can't I knit socks without dropping stitches?

You'll get the hang of it soon. Don't worry!

I can't.

You will, I promise.

Somehow one Mary couldn't convince the other that she was OK. But, with lots of encouragement, the negative Mary came around to believing she was more than OK and really very nice.

Aunt Anne understood, I realised, when Mum and I visited her in Glasgow. She was staying at the house where she lived as a girl. Her Dad had just died. She was wondering what to do with the place. It was very big, with precious pictures on all the walls. We walked through the front door, climbed the marble stairs, and found ourselves in a passageway with Anne's portrait painted at age five. She looked like Lewis Carroll's Alice, only Anne seemed more serious and her hair shorter and tidier. The artist was Sir William Nicholson. Anne's Dad was also a Sir. He inherited the title. Sir William earned his.

Mum told me that an artist painting a portrait tries to see into the sitter's soul. If this were true, what had Sir W seen behind Anne's, her well-ironed frock and expression? I'm sure he sensed a lonely, little girl with nothing surrounding her but dark furniture, dreary pictures and big windows. He wasn't fooled by the discomforting way she leant on a table covered with a dark brown cloth. She didn't smile. Her cheeks were flushed. Maybe she was wishing she was not so young: if she were older, she could tell that man with his paint brush to buzz off. She could stop having to pose. It was making her left leg stiff and giving her a crick in the neck. She longed to escape the artist's stare and go to her room to play with her mouse, the one she rescued from a trap set by the footman. She called it Timmy, and when she rescued another, trapped by her Dad's other footman, she called it Tammy, after the two men who tried to kill them: Tim Young and Tam Baird, who dressed like twins in the same clothes. Mum said they wore livery, which is another word for a uniform: with jackets edged in pink and trousers in ginger snap brown.

Off and on Tim and Tam played I-Spy with Anne at tea-time.

"I spy something beginning with M," began Tim.

"Mouse," suggested Tam.

"Milk," added Anne.

"Meringue," Tim suggested.

"Melting Moments, the biscuit!" shouted Anne.

Tim and Tam were serving the guests at a tea-party.

"Madeira cake!" Anne was delighted to find something else.

"What? Who's that?" asked her Dad who was hard of hearing.

"Mad-ear-a cake, Dad! Can't you hear?" Anne giggled.

"Muscovado syrup." Tam was pleased with himself.

"Not at tea-time! After dinner perhaps," warned Anne's Mum.

I never met Anne's parents. They were far too old by the time I was born but I imagined them like the King and Queen of Hearts in Alice in Wonderland. Really they were the King and Queen of Diamonds. They owned plenty of jewels, but not as many as a Maharajah. Mum said that the Nizam of Hyderabad had enough pearls to pave the streets of Piccadilly. "Where's that?" I asked. "Never mind!" said Mum.

Anne's Dad looked friendly enough, just like Alice's king who struck me as silly: he wore a crown over his wig.

"Why did the king wear both?" I asked. Judges wore wigs and kings, crowns. I knew.

"He wanted to judge people and rule them!" Dad scoffed.

"That's not fair. You must choose between one or the other."

Really the Queen in Alice in Wonderland was ghastly, ordering execution for anyone who disobeyed her. I knew, queens themselves got their heads chopped off, like Katherine Howard and Anne Boleyn. Kings too got beheaded. And one queen ordered Mary, Queen of Scots dead. Over in France, another lost hers in a guillotine. I wanted to tell the grumpy old Queen in Wonderland, if she wasn't careful she might lose hers too.

If Anne's Dad reminded me of a King card, her Mum was like the Queen. She may not have ordered executions but she was strict. "A no-nonsense type!" Mum told me.

In actual fact, Anne's mum was unwell. Most of her food had to be sieved or puréed.

"I can't eat anything lumpy!" she swore. So her diet was milk puddings, junkets, mashed potatoes, scrambled eggs and puréed carrots. Her bad stomach gave her a short temper, it seemed.

"It's so sore," she moaned, "I could swear a rat's gnawing at my insides." That was not a pleasant thought. I had seen a film of a beaver eating through a tree and the idea of one of those eating inside my tummy was very upsetting.

Surrounded by thick velvet curtains and beautiful antiques, Anne's Mum was determined not to let Anne become spoiled. She made her get up every morning at 7 oclock, take a cold bath and eat porridge with salt. "No sweets or trifles, for you, Miss!" she'd say. She stuck to that plan except at Christmas and on birthdays when Anne collected dozens of chocolates. But Anne longed for a dog. Her Dad had a pair of Springer spaniels, but she wanted her own. "If you really want one, you can get it from the dog and cat home," announced her Mum.

So, the chauffeur drove Anne to Corkerhill pound and there he was, a tan and white terrier whose right ear stood up while the other flopped over his left eye. She called him Corker and he followed Anne everywhere, inside the house and out. But one day on their favourite walk in the woods, he disappeared. Anne called for him and after a few minutes heard a muffled bark. Corker was stuck down a rabbit-hole. "Oh, no!" she wailed, remembering Alice in the story who landed at the bottom with a dreadful thump. For all Anne knew, this rabbit-hole was specially deep and ended in the ocean near Australia. she had heard of that country where bad Brits were once sent. But not any longer. She wanted to visit it to see kangaroos carrying their babies in their pouches.

"Oh, dear!" her Mum was alarmed. "I've lost at least two dogs like that and I never got them back!"

Anne began to weep.

"For heaven's sake, stop it. Otherwise you'll drown in your own tears. And you don't want to do that." Anne couldn't stop. But in no time, they were delighted to hear a loud bark and within a minute Corker's head, with one ear up, the other down, appeared from behind a rhododendron bush.

I wondered why Corker or anything else that belonged to Anne was not in her portrait. There were no dolls either — maybe her Mum never let her have any. Her Mum might have despised them, thinking girls shouldn't try to be so Mummyish. But, for the portrait, she could have let Anne hold a teddy, or her mouse, for that matter. But, no, she had to look grown up and sensible. Sir William instead painted in a straw hat with a grey ribbon round the crown, a pair of blue gloves, and a riding crop.

Anne liked to ride. Why ever not? Her pony was called Bullet because when you kicked him, he went like the wind round the farm, up by the hay-shed, along a dirt track close to the wood, and across a field. That's what she loved. To be free from her Mum and Dad, who reminded her of, not the King and Queen of Hearts, but of Clubs, with their orders: do this, do that, don't run in the house, close your mouth firmly when you chew, smooth down your dress in the drawing room, wash your hands before lunch, obey your elders, be polite, smile, and hold the door open for old Mrs X when she stumbles out of her room.

There was nothing Anne liked better than to snatch her hat and gloves from the cloakroom, run to the stables, saddle Bullet, scramble on to his back and canter down the track. With her pony's speed, she hardly needed her crop.

Tam and Tim taught her to play marbles and peevers, which Anne called hopscotch. "All you need is a couple o' flat stanes and chalk to mark the squares," Tim said.

Anne's Dad didn't like this. "It's best not to be too familiar with the footmen, Anne," he advised in his King of Clubs voice.

"Why?"

"Believe me, my child. Everyone has to know their place, in the scheme of things."

So, Anne befriended animals, who were less complicated. All they did was breathe, slobber, whine, bark, purr, slither, cheep or chirp. Anne added a new word to her M list: Menagerie. That's what she wanted: the best in the country. As she already had mice, she now collected flies, spiders, worms, and ear-wigs.

"No caterpillars, Anne!" Her Mum didn't want her to prevent them from turning into butterflies. Her Mum was concerned about birds too, as women wore hats with feathers. Everyone wore hats. It was rude not to, but the fashion went too far: the rich competed in wearing plumes from rare birds, not just peacocks and pheasants but egrets, humming birds, and hoopoes. Anne's Mum hated the custom and campaigned against it, by organising a march with a big placard, 'Feathers Crown Birds, not Women'.

Anne kept adding to her collection a hedgehog extracted from a pile of leaves the gardener had swept up for a bonfire; a rabbit saved from the keeper's gun; and a squirrel from the log shed. When she saw a starling with a damaged wing on the ledge of the nursery window, she scooped it up. Now she aimed to find an ark to fill with her animals. The idea came in church as the Minister told his congregation about Noah and the flood. Anne wondered how to fit in a giraffe and an elephant. Her house with its tall rooms was big enough, but she doubted her ark could hold all the animals. There was another problem too. She'd heard that Noah collected two of each kind. A he spider and a she; a he hedgehog and a she. Anne knew why. Her Mum didn't want her to but it was hard to stop her from knowing when she'd climb the gate at the farm and watch the cows in the field, after a farmer added his bull, but she never told her Mum and Dad what she saw. But the hardest thing for Anne was that she couldn't distinguish between a male ear-wig and a female, or a he sparrow from a she. As for fish, they seemed impossible. So, she gave up.

Whenever Mum was at the end of her rope, when Colin was teething and Lis and Janet fought, she'd phone Granny.

"Send Mary up on the plane. I'll have her for a week!"

There was no argument. I went. Mum drove me to Abbots Inch airport, and I boarded an airplane for Machrihanish in Kintyre. Sometimes my cousin, Nancy, was staying but more often than not, she'd gone home for the weekend. After climbing a steep hill, we arrived at Ballure, Granny's home where I met her friend, Dorothea. "What's your name, child?" she asked, like a Queen..

"I told you she's Mary, Esther's eldest," Granny explained.

At tea-time, in the dining room, Granny said that they hadn't time to wash up after lunch, and that was why we had to sit at the other end of the table, where the clean crockery lay.

"What happens when there are no more clean plates?" I asked.

"Don't be insolent, child!" complained Dorothea.

I didn't tell them but I thought, that this was the stupidest tea-time I'd ever been at. The truth was that Robert, Granny's cook, had his day off. Nobody washed the dishes because neither old lady knew how to. They'd always had someone to do it for them. By the time I'd finished eating a scone with butter and strawberry jam, I'd forgotten how frightening Granny and Dorothea were. Like Alice, I realised they were more like the Queens in a pack of cards. I needn't be afraid of them.

When Anne fetched me from Ballure to spend a day with her, I was happier. Alice had a sister and I had two. Anne had none. Whenever she noticed anyone on her own, lonely like her, she befriended the person. That's why she took the trouble to rescue me from Granny, when Mum made me stay there.

"Do you know," Anne said, "that a dog growls when it's angry and wags its tail when pleased, but a cat growls when it's pleased and wags its tail when angry. How's that for useless information?"

"Cats don't growl; they purr!" I said.

When I was at Aunt Anne's house, I had no wish, as I did at Granny's, to grow until I was nine feet tall. Anne let me feel OK at the size I actually was. It was odd that when she grew up, she did exactly the same as her Mum and Dad had done. She got an artist to paint a portrait of her young sons, John and Donald.

In it they wore kilts but no shoes or socks. This seemed strange because Anne was painted in a proper way wearing shiny black pumps and white socks, but for her sons' portrait, she wanted them to be bare-legged. It wasn't so surprising. Only two years previously Jock, their father, had his right leg blow off in France.

When I visited, at times Uncle Jock was there but usually he was with Betty, his secretary. If he was present, he never spoke. He held a Bible on his lap and read from it, ignoring everyone else in the room, including me. John and Donald didn't stay small or adorable for long. They grew up quickly, their fair hair turning mousey-brown and mostly they wore socks and shoes.

"Donald's coming home from school this evening, and he has a lot of spots. Please don't tease him," Anne announced one day when I was visiting. Both boys, who were a decade older than I, boarded at Winchester College in the south of England.

Everyone in the family thought John and Donald were much more important than me because they were rich and male while I didn't amount to much being a girl with a Dad not rich, which spurred me to take a swipe at Donald. His face looked like the surface of the moon with dozens of craters. I sort of said so.

In Primary three, Mrs Dunlop showed us a map of the world, pointing first to Europe. "Here we have the Alps. Mont Blanc is its highest peak." She told us about the Himalayas north of India.

I looked at Donald's face and across his left cheek was a row of white-tipped zits spoiling his pink skin. Running across his forehead were the Himalayas with an Everest of a spot in the center.

As for his chin, it had an impressive bump, also tipped in white, a wonderful Kilimanjaro of a plook. I tried not to smirk at the sight of my cousin, standing at the Aga rail. "Hello, Donald!" I said, giggling. "How are you?" He didn't answer.

"Why have you so many spots?" I jeered. Receiving no reply, I persisted. "Do you eat too much chocolate! Mum's told me it makes you get spots. Aren't you embarrassed you have so many?"

Anne looked disappointed. I felt bad. I'd betrayed her. I could not tell why I'd been so insensitive.

If Dad had been there, he would have been annoyed. "Be nice to your cousins," he often said. "If nothing else, they're rich."

"Why are they?" I asked.

"Because of Anne," he explained.

"Is she as rich as the Queen?"

"Nobody is."

"As rich as a duchess?"

"Some are poor. They've sold their tiaras just to eat."

"What are tiaras?"

"Alice bands of precious stones."

"Like a crown?"

"Sort of!"

"What if Aunt Anne sold her jewels?" I suggested.

"She never would."

"Why not?"

"Never get rid of your assets. If you do, you're finished. Kaput!"

One afternoon, Anne asked if I'd help with a special job. "A man is coming with his son to shoot at the Point!" she said.

The Point was rough ground close to the shore below Ballure. "I want you to be a beater."

That sounded nasty. Schoolmasters beat boys with canes, men beat dogs for chasing sheep. Why would I beat anything?

Anne explained, as if she read my mind. "I'll give you Jock's walking stick so you can beat the bushes and clumps of grass to frighten the birds into flying up into the air, so the shooters can take good aim at them."

I tried not to show Anne that I wasn't keen on doing this job, but, nobody, including Mum, let me disobey orders in the end.

"I'll tell you where to stand and when to beat the bushes to put up the duck!" Anne said.

When we reached the Point, I saw two men, dressed in dull green jackets and trousers only reaching to below their knees. Beneath these they wore thick socks the colour of snot and tough brown lace-up shoes. Mr. McVeigh, the gamekeeper, was there also, with whistles to call his dogs: a black Labrador and a spaniel.

"Here, you," he shouted at me. "Crouch down in that ditch and when the birds fly over, stand up, shout as loud as you can, and wave your arms in the air. That way they'll fly back into the guns."

So, I wasn't to beat the bushes to frighten the birds into flight. Instead, I was to make them change their path as if I were an aircraft controller of a busy airport. I'd never been asked to do this before. What if the birds flew too high to notice me stamping my feet and waving my arms like a lunatic?

I waited in the ditch, until I saw four duck flying towards me. I stood up, waved my arms in the air but was too embarrassed to shout. What was I supposed to yell, anyway? "Yoo-hoo, birdies. Don't fly over me; be good, little birdies and change direction so you get shot!" As I suspected, the duck didn't notice. I was tall but at nine years old, not that big. The birds flew over my head away from the guns. The keeper decided to end the shoot. "There's no more birds to be had!" he said, glaring at me. The man and his son gave me a dirty look too, but Anne smiled and said, "Well done, Mary! You saved the birds' lives!"

— THE CHASE —

WHY WAS I HERE, HUNTING? Sitting in a saddle on Marty's back at
the edge of the ploughed field, I could have turned away, but I
loved riding Marty, her quiet, little neigh and her coat of brown
and white patches. They were nothing like a leopard's spots, or
zebra's stripes, or a jaguar's blotches. Her markings were stars,
medallions, coins and maps of unknown continents. Beneath her
forelock was an elongated island. When I went to her stable and
groomed her, I got to know her every part: the patch on her right
flank, the slither of brown on her left foreleg, and the cluster
of coins on her belly.

We had stopped following the hounds. Why? I liked dogs, but
in a pack, they were different, as with people. It's easy to be
yourself on your own, but in a crowd you lose control and get
swept up in the moment, as with wolves and hyenas. I hadn't
thought carefully about what was to happen. I wondered, if I'd
lived in the time of public executions, would I also have dipped
my handkerchief in King Charles' blood, after he was beheaded?

Would I have gone to see a cock fight or a bear in a pit being
baited? At least in a bull-fight, the matador is really in danger. A
bull can gore and kill quick. He isn't always the sufferer.

When Mum read me Charles Dickens' 'A Tale of Two Cities', I
pictured the women by the guillotine, counting the victims:
"Crash! A head is held up and the knitting-women who scarcely
lifted their eyes to look...when it could think and speak, count..."
These women were characters in a novel, but they could be me,
my sister, or anyone, knitting while others get sacrificed. History
has lots of real stories.

On that afternoon, sitting on Marty's back, running my fingers
through her mane, I thought of the Paris women, needling
stitches of plain and pearl, not of wisdom but of blood. Pontius
Pilate came into my head too, the man who swore Christ did nothing wrong. "He's done nothing to me, so leave me alone," Pontius protested.

Why was I at the hunt then, not for company. I had few friends there, besides Marty. I enjoyed mucking out her stable, fetching the wheelbarrow, removing her droppings with a shovel, clearing the dirty straw, and replacing it with clean. I always gave her one part bran and one part bruised corn. Un-bruised corn causes colic in horses. I changed her water too, though carrying it in a bucket of galvanised steel was hard, it was so heavy, and I teased hay out of a bale, placing it in a rack, so she had no difficulty in eating it.

Paddy McDonald's cattle float had driven us to the hunt. Mum followed in the car. I wore my riding hat, the original black velvet turned dark green at the crown. I also had on Cousin Davina's old jodhpurs of thick cavalry twill. When they got wet, they chafed the insides of my legs. My jacket was a hand-me-down too.

In the old days, before Mr Darwin, Mr Marx and Dr Freud, I would've had to wait until my life was over before I was judged, but Mum says, we judge ourselves now. It's not so easy. At my age often, in each conflict, I split myself in two. Whatever I felt, my parents' voices still dominated, and Dad had encouraged me to believe it was okay to pony-gallop after a pack of dogs hell-bent on killing a fox. Dad stretched his long legs out before him. "You see, hunting's gone on for a long time!" He reminded me of the riding crop Aunt Jean had sent as a Christmas present. With it was a black felt belt with fabric sewn on in the shape of fox, hounds, and riders on horseback. The part of me that wanted approval liked it. It was pretty, and artful.

A few days before the hunt, I asked Mum if I should go. "Of course you should!" She was indignant. "You don't want to be a vegetarian?" To her, anyone disapproving of field or blood sports was a vegetarian. "And most are Socialists."

"And pacifists," Dad curled his upper lip.

Mum stretched herself to her full height. "I admire pacifists. Some are very principled and brave. In the Great War, they went out on the front line with stretchers to rescue the wounded. It's the people who profit from war I object to. Anyway, Mary, you can't be vegetarian. We all prey on each other, don't we?"

"That's Nature, red in tooth and claw." Dad was polishing off a big slice of roast beef at our Sunday lunch. Mum followed with her favourite: "Take the fox. He kills for fun, rampaging through hen-houses, slaughtering everything in sight," she said, grasping her knife and fork.

Dad stretched a long arm for the gravy boat. "A very slippery customer, if there ever was one. Beatrix Potter got it right! Her fox tricked silly Jemima Puddle duck, who was female."

Dad smirked at Mum who was urging Lis to eat her Yorkshire pudding. "And it serves as a timely warning to young girls of the fate awaiting them if they're too trusting..."

"of faithless men!" snapped Mum.

If it was alright for hounds to kill a fox, what happened if the dogs scented a hare?

"They're fox hounds, they're not supposed to kill them!"

"They might!"

"It's a risk you have to take!"

I'd no wish to do that. Breck once killed a doe hare in the field by the river. She noticed it by the hedge, nursing its young, a sitting target. I couldn't forget the sight of the dead mother and her leverets.

I liked hares. With a heart far bigger than a rabbit's, it's almost as swift as a lion. Rabbits crowd together in underground burrows, a hare shelters above ground in a depression; its young are born fully furred with their eyes open, unlike a newborn rabbit, which is bald and has closed eyes. A hare's iris is orange, not dark brown like a rabbit's. The previous March, I came across a hare, all legs and ears, that looked as mad as the one in 'Alice in Wonderland'; Boxing clever, the hare is a far cry from its cousin who runs for cover down a hole in the earth. The hare is daring, undefended, a loner, taking its chances in furrow, field and ditch. It explores and lives dangerously, 'building its cities on the slopes of Vesuvius', as a book put it, that Aunt Anne gave me.

Dora liked but feared them. "If one o' them crosses his path, my Dad doesny go fishing. He stays in the hoose a' day. Some folk think they're witches. I mind how my Aunty Mabel said at full moon, hares turn into bonny women who hurry the spring in after the winter. Mrs MacColl tellt me hares care for the dead and lead them from this world into the next."

Dora's favorite story was of a warrior who wounded a hare in the leg. Following it into a wood, he found himself in an underground hall standing before a beautiful woman on a throne but wounded in the leg. At school I avoided telling Mrs Dunlop Dora's hare stories. "Stuff and nonsense!" she might say. "All mumbo jumbo, but keep away from those beasts. They have the evil eye."

At the hunt, it rained but nobody took cover or complained. I felt uncomfortable, but it wasn't smart to wear a waterproof over your jacket, far less cover your riding hat with a hood. I heard a hound cry or 'give voice'? The others looked up with excitement. Sylvia Campbell close to me, on her New Forest pony, stuffed the remains of her ham sandwich in her mouth and raised herself in her stirrups. Soon all twenty-four dogs were barking; the din was unbelievable and every bit as deafening as a squadron of planes flying overhead. I never liked that sound, but I went along with it and, like Sylvia, pretended excitement, even pleasure, at the chase. The Master in his red jacket blew his horn and away we galloped down a lane, across a field and into a wood where we jumped over a fallen tree and across a ditch. By a clump of beeches, the dogs killed. I didn't see the exact spot, but that was it. We were all tired and turned back heading for the big house where the hunt began.

"Here, you!" the Master shouted at me as he bent over the dead animal, knife in hand. "This is your first kill, isn't it?" I glanced at Mum standing beside Mrs Campbell and wondered who was most frightening: the man in the red jacket or Mum in disappointment if I rebelled.

"Don't make a fuss, Mary!" she often said. "Keep quiet and be polite! Just swallow it! The last thing we want is a fuss! Be a good girl and don't complain! Put up and shut up. Understand?"

She nodded in approval watching the man dip his forefinger inside the animal's head. Without ceremony he daubed my right cheek, then my left with the blood. "Don't wash it off till bedtime!" he warned as he shoved the bloody, furry bundle into my hand. Someone else helped me tie the creature's neck to the ring on the back of my pony's saddle, and now it was time to return home. I trotted down the road to Paddy McDonald's cattle float, the head bouncing in unison with my pony's stride. The Master called a severed head a 'mask'. Like the knitting women, who counted heads as they rolled from the guillotine, the Master saw the hare as a quantity, not a living creature.

The hunters were pleased with the hounds. They'd have preferred a fox, but a hare was alright. Johnny on the piebald got the tail or 'brush' and Sylvia a paw or 'pad', as the Master called it. In the rain, the hare's blood ran in rivulets down my pony's flank. I willed myself to be proud. It was an honour to claim the head. Dad told me I could have it stuffed so that glass eyes would replace the real ones. Hunters did that. A taxidermist helped. He made dead animals look as if they were alive.

Back home, I wrote 'taxidermist' in my notebook and planned. Beneath the stuffed head attached to a wooden plaque I'd put my name and the date the hare was killed. Also the name of the hunt. I had to be pleased. Hunting was what we did. It prepared us for life, for controlling our world. It was normal, after all. Didn't Mum say so? "When I was your age I liked nothing better than to watch them geld the rams in the stackyard." Really? She enjoyed seeing sheeps' balls cut off?

I fed Marty with a large portion of bruised corn and gave her fresh water to drink. I brushed her down, making sure her belly markings, the guineas, shillings and pennies and the island below her forelock were free from mud. I even polished her saddle and bridle, applying Brasso to the bit and stirrups, but that night I couldn't sleep. I tossed and turned: two Marys argued with each other. I didn't like their discussion.

Dad had a way of stopping disagreement with him or anyone else. When we ignored his wishes, he'd introduce a conversation-stopper. "Do you know what I saw this morning?" he would ask.

"No!" we shouted.

"A blackbird. It was flying upside down and...."

"Doing slow rolls and..."

"Stop it, Lizzie," he ordered. "We don't want vulgarity at the dining table! I hate arguments, you know that!"

I didn't like arguments either, especially between myself.
Two Marys tussling made me frightened and tired.

    I won't go hunting again.

    Why not?

    I can't bear to see another hare killed.

    Will you go if it's a fox instead?

    How can I be sure it won't be another hare?

    That's the risk you take.

    I don't want to go, even if it's a fox.

    But foxes kill hens and ducks, for fun.

    So do humans.

    Don't be difficult. We hunt and shoot to cull the animals
or there'd be too many and they'd die of starvation.

    Culled or killed, what's the difference?

    As you like eggs, the next time a fox raids a hen-house,
ask the farmer why he hasn't any for you to eat.

After the argument, I fell asleep and into a nightmare. I was at a hunt on Marty. We followed the Master and the hounds down the edge of a field, I saw the hare, its long ears pinned back, crouching in a decline. The lead hound caught its scent and the raucous baying began. The hare plunged into a ditch. The hounds followed. I turned my head away, unable to watch. "Bravo!" cried the woman on a grey horse behind me. "Well done, hounds!" We all returned to the farm where the hunt had met that morning. The Master beamed as he presented the woman with the hare's head, a freckled boy with a paw and after distributing the remaining three, he came up to me. "No foxes for you today, Miss, but here's the bunny's tail. Pin it on your wall at home."

"I don't want that tail!" I screamed. "Nor any other part of the animal your dogs killed."

I turned towards Mum. "Take me home," I said. "At once!"

"Now leave me, please!" she announced. "I must end my chapter."

Mum had given our visitor the bedroom looking out on to the field, where the cows gorged on young grass, daisies, and buttercups. The lady didn't close her door so I stood in the passage-way and peered in. On a chair by the dressing table was her brown leather case, its lid already open. Bending over it, she rummaged through her dresses, blouses and knitwear until she found a woolen cardigan in russet brown, which she put on, and a wad of paper. I'd seen Granny's writing pad of azure sheets but these were larger and whiter. Holding her fountain pen, the lady sat down at a square table, originally a games table but now plain furniture holding an electric lamp and a vase of flowers. Beside these, our guest laid out her paper and began to write. I couldn't take my eyes off her. It was her sense of purpose that impressed. I was mesmerised by the movement of her pen. How could she write so fast and with such confidence? I'd never seen Mum so enthusiastic about anything except perhaps when she viewed an unfamiliar bird like a goosander or widgeon, but she was always bemoaning their lack of variety at Carsenestock; so it was a turn-up for the books if she came across a bird out of the ordinary.

"Have you seen a hoopoe, this season?" Dad would joke.

"Hardly!" Mum replied, "But if any arrive, which is highly unlikely, they'll fly south, not up here."

Our visitor was the novelist Mary Anne O'Malley, who wrote under the name of Anne Bridge. A friend of Granny, she also knew my other grandmother, Dad's mum, and gone on a skiing holiday with them in 1933, while Dad was a Cambridge undergraduate. I'd seen a photo of her in one of his albums, standing next to him in St. Moritz.

After reading Mary-Anne's novel, 'An Illyrian Spring', Mum realised that it was published not long after that holiday in Switzerland. She was intrigued by the character, an unhappily married woman, who meets on holiday, a sad young man, who is thwarted by his oppressive father from becoming an artist.

On the morning following Mary Anne's arrival, before she came down for breakfast and while Dad was consulting Bob Young in the byre, Mum took me into her confidence. "I think she's still sweet on Dad."

"Who?"

"Mary Anne. I told you about her novel with the miserable young man forbidden to become an artist and how an older woman falls in love with him. She's based her plot on Dad when she met him in St. Moritz in 1933!"

"You're joking!"

"Didn't you know that your grandfather threatened to cut Dad off without a penny if he became an artist."

"I can't believe she'd use Dad in that way..."

"Can't you? Novelists are notorious for that kind of thing. They're like magpies; they steal."

"I suppose Dad was quite handsome when he was young."

"Yes. Very!"

"How did Mary Anne become a writer?"

"She was married to a diplomat and wherever he was posted, she went with him, writing about the places they visited. Her best-known book, that won a prize in America, was about Peking's foreigners during the twenties. They had a whale of a time, living it up, not caring much about the Chinese, who were caught up in a civil war."

Mum sat down with her toast, to pour herself a cup of coffee. "Do you know, I never thought about it but maybe the O'Malleys knew Uncle Lewis in China!"

The door opened to reveal our guest, dressed in dark slacks, as she called them, a roll-neck top of beige brushed cotton and the same cardigan I saw her pull from her case the previous evening.

"Hello, Esther!" she trilled.

"Good morning, Mary Anne! Did you sleep well?"

"Like a top! Lovely air you have here!"

"Sit down and I'll get you..."

"Just cornflakes and a cup of coffee, please!"

Once they were both seated, Mum posed her question.

"Did you know my uncle, Lewis Crabbe, in China?"

"You know, the ex-pat community was very small!" Mary Anne glanced at Mum before she dropped two sugar lumps into her coffee. "I met everyone worth knowing there but I don't think..."

Mum pursed her lips and bit angrily into a corner of her toast. "Really?" she murmured.

I was upset that our visitor thought my great-uncle wasn't worth knowing. If, as a rear-admiral, he wasn't, would she have acknowledged him had he been a front-admiral, in the same way that a car had front and rear lights?

Mary Anne wasn't our only visitor. Dozens more descended, mostly Granny's friends who, after staying with her, came to us; many were married to colonels, brigadiers, generals or diplomats. Widowed for a long time, Granny relied on these women for company and at the least opportunity would fill her house with them. Dorothea Russell, wife of Cairo's police chief, before and during the war, was one.

"She wears suits by Worth!" Mum declared.

"Is that worth it?" I was being facetious.

"Only the slimmest of women suit...."

"these suits?"

"I call them a coat and skirt," said Mum snobbishly.

"Oh, well!"

"During the war, Dorothea started a club in Cairo called 'Music for All'. There was nothing for the soldiers to do there except..."

"Get drunk and, well, you know..."

Dad cleared his throat.

"So she got the troops to listen to classical music in an old Cairo cinema," explained Mum.

"I ask you," scoffed my Dad. "As if those Tommy's swallowed Mozart and Bach. God knows what would have happened if she had subjected them to Wagner!"

Mum was defiant. "I think she was very enterprising. There were over 140,000 British troops in Cairo, twiddling their thumbs in their spare time and many of them loved classical music."

"I suppose she gave the Eye-ties the thumbs down!"

"The what's?"

"The Italians...you know...Puccini, Verdi, Mascagni."

"How should I know, but she obviously found composers to entertain them."

I still found Mary Anne the most impressive visitor because she wrote novels, not just while she was at home but in houses like ours where she finished chapters in her bedroom, in hotel rooms, railway carriages and even in dentists' waiting rooms.

Mum preferred to invite gardeners, women with green fingers and weather-beaten faces. When Great-Aunt Iris stayed, she loved weeding the garden. "Give me something to kneel on," she said, "and I'll get it in order. Then, when I come in, you can hand me a glass of sherry."

"But Aunt Iris, we live on pure clay," Mum warned. "Bone dry in summer, squelching in winter."

"Never mind! It's perfect for roses. You'll just have to say good-bye to heathers and rhododendrons."

While Mary Anne was the real thing, a published author with a pseudonym and awards, Great Aunt Conty was not. She refused to travel north of the Border, so I never discovered if she'd have chased me out of her room to finish writing her chapter. Conty wrote books with silly titles. I don't know if she meant 'Frolic Youth' to be ironical but the memoir chronicles the Edwardian upper classes enjoying themselves before the great cull when most of the young men she knew were slaughtered in Flanders. 'Smile at Time' depicts her early years. 'Flowers and Elephants' describes Conty's exploits as part of 'The Fishing Fleet' (the name for a young woman seeking a husband) in India during the Raj. Conty did find and marry General Sitwell, thirty years her senior but unlike his cousins, Edith, Osbert and Sacheverel, he wasn't as literary. Conty tried to make up for this lack by self-publishing her memoirs under her married name until Edith suggested she stop.

"Your books undermine ours," she protested. During their youths, Edith and Conty were friends until the two young women were forced to choose between marriage or literature. Unable to enjoy both, plain Edith plumped for poetry and the single life while pretty Conty chose marriage and little literary distinction.

Each Christmas, Conty sent Dad a copy of her latest work.

Not reading it, he ridiculed it instead, lampooning the title. 'Flowers and Elephants' 'Farts and Heffalumps'! 'Frolic Youth', 'Rollicking spoof'! 'Smile at Time', 'Smoke my Woodbine'! Dad was a passed master, not so much at the pun or retort, but at good nonsense language. He loved babbling a string of unintelligible words. "Mullard Sylbill ticky-tacky pix pox," was one he used as an endearment for us or the cat. He would grasp it by the tail, lift it on to his lap and whisper into its ear. "What do you want, Civet cat? Willy-wiley, tracksy, tacksy, feline, felonious, fixity fax-cat?"

His favourite Victorian was Edward Lear, whose nonsense poems and Quangle-Wangle, Pobble, and Jumblies heroes, he adored. Whenever we had mince for lunch he would recite the second verse of 'The Owl and the Pussycat'.

> They dined on mince and slices of quince
> Which they ate with a runcible spoon.
> And hand in hand, on the edge of the sand,
> They danced by the light of the moon...

"What's a runcible spoon?" asked Lis.

"Dunno! It isn't important, it's the sound of it that matters. Dad repeated the word several times, rolling the 'r' and exploding the 'b' between his lips.

Edward Lear wrote plenty of limericks but they were never bawdy. Likewise, Dad wasn't particularly rude in his conversation except for an occasional reference to bodily functions like flatulence. He liked playing with Lear's limericks too and changing the words: '...the old man of Aosta, who possessed a large cow but lost her,' became 'there was an old man of the Cree who had a large cow but set her free...'

After Dad demolished his aunt's titles, he tore apart her prose. "She can't spell and as for her punctuation, it's elementary at best, non-existent at worst." He mocked her romantic scenes, reading them aloud in a gasp: "He gazed at me with admiration.

'How lovely you look this evening. How Beguiling!'"

Oddly, Dad saw more than a likeness of Conty in me. At mealtimes, if I asked about the weather or for someone to pass the salt, or even how to fix an electric plug, Dad chuckled. "You sound like Aunt Conty," he remarked.

"How do I?"

"The way you turn your head and look out of the window, and your tone of voice is similar. Loopy, but strangely alert!"

I wasn't pleased to be identified with a great-aunt I'd never met, a woman cruelly ridiculed by her nephew. Was this his way of corralling me into convention? I now saw Dad's attitude towards Conty as representing our family's way of dealing with women who deviated from the norm.

"Who is she anyway?" I asked.

"My mother's sister!" Dad explained.

"And a free spirit!" Mum suggested.

"You can say that again!" he laughed. "She was certainly all spirit!"

"What do you mean?"

"She's a spiritualist lately!"

"A what?"

"A person who contacts the dead."

"How weird!"

"It is. Barmy, actually!"

"Very dangerous!" added Mum. "Granny once practised table-turning and got a nasty fright. She never tried it again."

"People can go mad doing things like that."

"Is Conty mad?"

"Eccentric, but not actually mad. With her spiritualism, she's met some interesting people like W B Yeats, the Irish poet. So, maybe it's not so bad that you bear a resemblance to her," Dad said. I wasn't so sure. Spirits weren't what I needed. I wanted to contact the living.

With all these literary connections in the family, I began to think I could write too. So, I climbed the stairs up to the guest room, closed the door so that Lis and Janet couldn't come in,

102

and began to try it out.

"Leave me be," I shouted through the door. "I'm writing my novel!"

"A likely story!"

"You'll see. I'll show you!"

"Will you?" I heard them retreat down the stairs as I dumped my notebook and pencil on to the square table by the bed.

Then there was Granny's visits. Before she came Mum and Dad erected wire netting over the outside of each ground floor window to prevent farm cats entering our house. Granny had a cat phobia. You could say, she had a Lis, Janet and me phobia also. She was not overly fond of us, except for our brother, whom she liked but we weren't sure why. Strangely, she expressed affection and concern for us but only on paper in letters to Mum. If we weren't her favorite grandchildren nor Mum her favorite daughter, duty still demanded she take an interest in us, so she visited us from time to time, and made us read out aloud passages from our school books, help untangle her knitting wool, clean the silver or weed part of the garden where there were no alpines or herbaceous plants that we could pull up. She even taught us Patience played with two packs, which was impossibly difficult. If we played her game of button our lip, feign cheerfulness, and disregard feelings, she approved. I felt and cared too much about what she thought, unfortunately.

One day, while Granny was with us, I discovered that a comic called 'Girl' was inviting readers to take part in a competition. 'Write a story,' it announced, 'no more than 250 words about a special day in your life.' It gave an address for sending. The prize was £25 and a year's subscription. I wasn't too worried because, to be truthful, I didn't think I had a chance of winning but I wanted nonetheless to enter a story. The competition was right up my street. I was thrilled by the thought; I could write stories about my life disguised as fiction. With a notepad and pencil, I climbed the stairs to be alone and to concentrate. The guest room was out of bounds because Granny occupied it so, after supper, I settled for my own room. Peering out of the window at the hill, I saw a sickle moon hovering above. Dora had told me that under its influence, good luck came to the start of a new project.

My story was about a young girl who rode a skewbald pony called Tarmy, an anagram for Marty. The first sentence was hard but I found my voice in the second. By the time I'd written a whole page I was galloping along, but, as soon as I finished counting the words, I realised it was one hundred over the limit and the competition's closing date was in three days' time.

"What shall I do?" I wailed in the kitchen where Mum was preparing a chicken casserole for supper.

"Give it to me!" Granny said, holding out her palm. "I'll fix it!"

I wasn't keen to let my 'baby' be cared for by such a nursemaid. She might pummel it out of recognition or even kill it.

"Come on! I'll sort it out!" she said in an authoritative voice. So I gave her my scribbles and watched her making corrections to the script. Each time I saw her seated in an armchair by the fire in the sitting room, I noticed the fistful of paper on her lap and wondered if it was mine or a letter she was writing to a friend or relative. So, I stole myself to find out. "Did you finish shortening my story, Granny?" I asked. I suspected she had scribbled all over it with red pencil, corrected the spelling and cut out the 'ands', 'buts' and 'thens'? Maybe she had introduced paragraphs, which I never knew how to do. She may even have cut my story into strips, chewed up the pieces, and spat them out, for all I knew.

I got no answer. The following evening when I saw Granny again with a pad of paper on her lap and pen in hand, I asked again. "Did you send off my story, Granny?" .

"Be quiet, I'm trying to concentrate!" she barked.

As editors went, Granny was not only the first but my worst. She never returned my manuscript. I never heard what happened to it either.

Happily at least, my independence of mind and courage to speak my thoughts soon earned Mum's approval. I became her mouth-piece, expressing what she dared not say herself. Sometimes I defended her in an argument with Dad and now even challenged Granny. One morning, I went straight to the point, as near as I could in our genteel way. Once again, Granny scolded me hard for banging the kitchen door and not laying the dining table properly. "The spoons should go here, not there, but HERE!" she said. "Whoever heard of them going THERE?"

Thinking this over, I realized that if I'd belonged to another family, I would have screamed at her and told her where to get off but good behaviour and maturity beyond my years, were expected of us. So I attempted a more subtle tack. "When are you leaving, Granny?"

The shock, registering on her face, was palpable. For a moment she was at a loss for words.

"On Tuesday! And what business is it of yours?"

"Because you're upsetting me!" I replied. I would have loved to have told my grandmother that she was a nasty, old witch but I didn't have an adult way to describe my childish feelings. Had I been older, I might have excused her as an old lady, afraid, lonely, unwell and grieving for a son killed during the war and concerned for another, who was badly wounded.

After Granny left, Mum reminded me of how well I had defied her. Preferring to take shelter behind another whenever flak flew, Mum loved to see me spike pomposity and cut through the hypocrisy. As her foot soldier I dared to stick my head over the parapet but when missiles approached, she took cover and failed to minister bandages, contrary to what she had done during the war.

Esther Moreton Macdonald
Gladstone: Mum

I'VE ALREADY MENTIONED, that in the spare room there stood an old square table with a detachable top that served as a drafts or chess board. Where the pieces had got to was anyone's guess. We never played those games as nobody in the family knew how to.

Beneath the table-top was a space for backgammon but we were ignorant of the rules so we avoided that activity too. In my imagination, the games table was for Regency bucks, swash-buckling roués straight out of a Georgette Heyer novel. One or two of Mum and Dad's ex-colonial friends and relatives, however, played Mah-Jong and, of course, a contingent of Wigtownshire worthies met regularly to play a very serious game of Bridge.

These amusements were too cerebral for us; my parents were well-educated, but didn't give the impression as their upbringings discouraged them from flaunting their minds. After attending Cambridge for a year, Dad studied at the Architectural Association and, on gaining entry to Somerville College, Oxford, in 1939, Mum threw up the opportunity because of a World War. Never-theless, when someone displayed ignorance, especially in art or literature, they expressed dismay, even shock. "Do you know that Cyril Bracken believed a Raeburn was a kitchen stove?" Dad scoffed. To him, all educated people should have known that Raeburn was a famous Scottish portrait painter. Dad had little interest in literature, particularly Shakespeare, but sometimes he quoted from the bard. When I fought with him, he would hiss, 'Terrible it is to have an ungrateful daughter!'"

That he gave gravitas to his anger by quoting a line from King Lear amused me. For someone who claimed he knew little about the written word, Dad kept a well-stocked pile of quotations handy. But I wasn't ignorant either. I knew which play he had chosen for his ammunition.

"You know what Lear was, don't you?" I asked.

"What, then?"

"A stupid old fool!"

On receiving my outburst of insubordination, Dad hesitated

for a couple of seconds, then lowered his shoulders and mouthed, "Touché!"

This was his response whenever a riposte succeeded over his lunge. He might be a master at verbal combat but his admissions of defeat were expressed in French, of course.

Dad never understood how clever people could read trash. He disdained our family doctor, who was clever, but read the Daily Express. "I ask you," Dad shook his head, "The Daily Express!"

Our card games were equally simple. 'Snap' was a favourite, particularly with the young ones. It was about finding identical cards. If you uncovered a Queen, you had to upturn its equivalent: a Queen for a Queen, or a King for a King. Finding the partner, instantly you shouted 'Snap!'

It was similar in Nature. If you noticed a magpie, you might exclaim, 'One for sorrow, two for joy!' Breeding was paramount; loners weren't needed. Snap was a password to partnership and even coupledom.

Like Snap, Pelmanism was another game for us to recognize patterns and to test our memories. Placing the whole pack of cards on a table face down, you picked one and tried to find its partner. Younger players were often better at this than the adults.

Other games were stacked with obvious innuendo. We owned a special pack for playing Happy Families. It had Daddies who wore bowlers and carried brief-cases and brollies while Mummies dressed in frilly aprons. Our pack had a dozen families with names describing the Daddy's profession like Mr Bone, the fat and rosy-faced butcher, Mr Flour, the baker, Mr Pint, the milkman, Mr Saw, the carpenter, and Mr Wheel, the carter. Miss Bone had flaxen hair in pigtails and her mother held a string of pork sausages. Mr Chutney, the grocer, reminded me of the brown overalled Willie Paterson from Kirkcowan, who drove in his large van to our back door each Saturday. He acted his part perfectly with his round face, sugary voice, and wide smile. We never saw the real Mrs Paterson. I imagined her daughter was like Miss Chutney, a dark-haired, spicy looking girl with a sallow complexion, who looked like a pixie in a forest, and the Patersons' son as similar to Master Chutney, a fast talker in a tweed cap who resembled the chimney sweep played by Dick van Dyke in the Mary Poppins movie.

By no stretch of the imagination could one card of the pack be associated with a family of any kind. This was the Old Maid. Her card was frightening and we shuddered at the sight of her in our hand. Colin referred to her as 'the home maid' while Dad called her 'the dairy maid'. Dressed in a long, black coat, she looked grim, with lace-up boots and a rolled-up umbrella in her right hand. A pince-nez balanced on the bridge of her nose, and a tight-fitting bonnet enveloped her head. The worst part of the game was at the beginning, when the whole pack was placed face down on the table. Each card looked the same. Admittedly, one or two were dog-eared, others were nicked along the edges, or even torn and bent. Everyone, however, knew which card was the Old Maid as it was, by far, the most bent and grubby. Once, when Dad dealt the card to Lis, she tried to hide it by sitting on it. Another time, Janet folded it into quarters so she could stuff it up the sleeve of her cardigan. For some reason, best known to Dad, I was often dealt the Old Maid, a witch in waiting.

"Oh, bad luck, Mary! Very bad!" Dad exclaimed. He believed in ill luck, and was convinced he had it more than anyone he knew. "Oh, my gosh, you are unlucky, Mary, to get that horrible card! How can you cope with being the Old Maid again? Lord Luck, that's all it is if you really want to know!" As soon as Dad adopted this mode of thinking, we knew we were in for a series of sad memories. "You know what it's like!" He shot his chin towards the ceiling, gazed out of the window and mumbled, "Once, I had jaundice during the war and..." I knew the story by heart. "my bomber crew went up with someone else and never came back."

"Who were they, Dad, your crew?"

"What were their names?"

Either he didn't hear us or refused to answer. "It was luck, Lord Luck! That's all," he insisted. "Good or bad, you never know until it's too late!" he said angrily.

In spite of the fact that he'd been lucky not to be killed, he still felt aggrieved. "I should have been made a wing commander. In North Africa, I did the work of someone of that rank, after all, but my boss was from New Zealand, and he passed me up for promotion when ..." his voice trailed off into a lugubrious silence.

It troubled me that life turned sour for so many. Fairy stories had happy endings. Cinderella got her prince, Hansel and Gretel were saved from the wicked witch, Snow white was found and The Sleeping Beauty woke from her sleep, and elsewhere distant relatives left unexpected legacies in the nick of time. Inheritances abounded and generosity arrived. All's well in the best of possible worlds and everyone lives happily ever after, but Dad was all but disinherited and as the fifth child, and an after-thought, Mum was virtually ignored by her family. I wanted, if not a fairy godmother, then a nice aunt or long-lost cousin to come up trumps for me. I may have been the eldest, but I was female and in families like mine, that was damnation itself. Yet, my belief in good persisted.

Still I complained about being lumbered with more than my fair share of the dreaded card, Dad urged my tolerance. "Come on, Mary. Remember, you're the oldest, so take it on the chin! You can cope with it, can't you?...Oh, dear! You're old maid again. What a horrible thought. Do you know, no woman in the family has ever been an old maid. Maybe you'll be the first, Mary!" Dad milked it so much, I felt angry, but it was oddly intriguing to think of myself as coming first in anything even if it was an ignominious 'first past the post' for my family. When all was said and done, why shouldn't I become an old maid? What was wrong with never marrying? As it stood, most Mums and Dads I knew weren't fairy tale happy, anyway. As for having children, I had enough younger ones to deal with already.

Apart from games whose winners relied more on luck than skill, we tried our hand at Racing Demon. Each of us scurried through our individual packs of cards like hamsters turning a wheel, followed by a series of thumps when the winner and the opponent banged the cards on to the pile. Cards flew into the air, were torn, bent and scrunched into a ball, as each player fought to come first. We played on our dining table, a mock, Georgian, oval affair with lion's claw feet, that came apart in the middle and fell into two halves. To play our game, Mum covered the top with a thick cotton bed-spread.

"We'll have to get a proper card table!" Dad said, after the cover slipped off the table and fell on to the floor. A week later, it arrived in a large furniture van. The driver deposited it in its box at the back door. Dad carried it into the television room. When he opened the box, he brought out a collapsible table. "It's made of cloth," said Dad stroking the green fabric top.

"Is it felt?" I asked.

"No! It's called baize, a coarse woolen material, I think. Do you know what 'the green baize door' is?" he asked.

I shook my head.

"In the old days in big houses, when the family didn't want to hear the crashing of pots and pans, they tacked this cloth on to their kitchen or pantry doors to deaden the noise.

Now that we had a table of green baize specifically for card games, we played everything on it. When it came to stowing it away after the game, in a niche between the wall and the side of a Jacobean-style book-case, presented to Mum by friends on the occasion of her marriage, nobody knew how to collapse it or fold the legs into the underside of the table-top.

"Press here! Up at the top, silly!" Mum urged. "Here!" She pointed to a black square at the top of the leg. "Oh, for goodness sake, can't you get the hang of the thing?" she persisted.

"No. I can't!" Dad pushed, poked and tried to coax the leg into action but nothing could persuade the table-leg to fold over.

"Get the manual, David!"

"I've no idea where it is. I never read them!"

"Well, if you leave the table lying upside down like this, its legs will break."

Eventually they managed it. "It's on a spring," announced Mum as she folded triumphantly the legs into the underside of the table-top. "How silly of us not to get that straightaway!"

I WAS WITH DORA in the passageway helping her dust the family portraits, mainly copies of originals and of little money value.

"She's weird!" Dora said, turning with her feather duster to a portrait of Dad's distant ancestress, Anne Dashwood.

"What do you mean?" I peered at a black and white print of a woman dressed as a shepherdess, holding a crook though nobody could be fooled by her get-up, with rubies and pearls around her neck and a silk, gauze scarf draped over her shoulders.

"It's her bust! It's way too high, right above her oxters. That's a high-waister she's wearing," Dora said, "with a low neckline. Not plunging! Just low and her bust's bare," she added with disgust, holding her feather duster like a stick about to come down hard on the glass. "I dinny understand how she could keep it up."

"What?"

"Her bust. I could swear they didny wear bras, then!" Dora shook her head.

I had little interest in bras. I didn't need one; at least, not yet.

Dora couldn't take her eyes off the print. "Maybe she's hiked up her tits so they fit into her bodice. A shepherdess, did you say? Wi' a crook and a wee lamb at her heels, is that what it is?"

Dad hung all his paintings at his eye level which was very high. Dora stood on tip-toe and peered again at the picture; "mair like a poodle, to my mind. Get away with you! You couldny see her in yon dress clipping and dipping sheep, howking tatties or milking the cows."

"Mum told me it was the fashion, then, for rich ladies to wear poor women's clothes and pretend." I said gingerly.

Dora dropped the feather duster and creased up with laughter. "You don't say! The wealthy are ae like that. It's a game to them to act poor!"

When Dad found this print in a pile of family papers, he got Mr Edwards in the photograph shop to make a gilt frame for it. He pinned a plaque on the bottom: 'Anne Dashwood, Countess of Galloway, David Steuart Gladstone's third cousin, four times removed, who owned Carsenestock.' The idea behind Dad's explanation was not so much snobbery but a desire to stress that our farm had once been owned by a member of the family.

Anne Dashwood looked too pleased with herself for me to like her. I wouldn't have wanted to be her friend, sister or daughter: far worse, her maid. I had an inexplicable urge to grab her hair and pull it particularly as it was arranged in bunches, not pigtails, like Melanie's until her Mum cut them off. Most irritating was the patterned scarf that fell over Anne Dashwood's bodice 'wi her tits hanging oot', as Dora had said. If it was designed to conceal them, instead it accentuated them.

At school Mr Godfrey, our new teacher, told us: "Everyone should know about their past! That's why we study the French Revolution."

"We're not French," said my neighbour, Jock Wallace.

"It doesn't matter! That cataclysmic event affected the whole of Europe!" Mr Godfrey didn't care if he bamboozled us with such unintelligible words.

"They had a Queen called Marie Antoinette," he explained, "who was Austrian but married to Louis, the French king. Before the Revolution, she dressed up and pretended to be a milk-maid. It was the fashion, then."

I wondered, why Anne Dashwood would follow the French Queen's example, when she knew what had happened to her.

"Now, boys and girls," asked Mr Godfrey, "do you know how Marie Antoinette died?

"They cut off her head just like they did with Mary Queen of Scots," piped up my erstwhile friend, Melanie Fraser.

"That's true but how did they cut it off?"

"With an axe!" said Sam McWhirter. "What else, stupid?"

"With a guillotine!" said Mr Godfrey who apparently hadn't heard Sam's remark. "Can you spell it?" he turned to the blackboard with his chalk. It was almost as hard as spelling Kirkcudbright, a town near Newton Stewart. Mr Godfrey had taught us to spell this word by dissecting it into three parts. "Now, the final part of the word is easy, isn't it? It's 'bright'. We all know what that means and we all wish to be bright at our studies, don't we, only some of us are not?" said Mr Godfrey, staring straight at Sam McWhirter.

This portrait of Anne Dashwood was my second least favourite. At the bottom of the list was a painting in the passageway to the left of the door into the sitting room, of an old man who looked like a frightening bird. "This," Dad announced, "is a portrait of William Ewart Gladstone, your first cousin twice removed."

I was quite small when I first saw the picture. In my eye, the man looked too old to be my cousin. As for being twice removed, I couldn't work that out at all. "It's about different generations," was Dad's inadequate explanation.

Each time I clutched the staircase rail to climb up to my room, I caught sight of the grey-haired figure dressed in black. "During Victoria's reign," said Dad, "he was Prime Minister four times!"

I'd seen politicians speak on television but I never listened to what they said. To be a prime minister four times, was impressive nonetheless. All I'd done four times was win the three-legged race with Lis at the Sunday School picnic, for four years running.

The picture was gigantic; it stretched from just above a table to nearly the ceiling. Dad had ordered a copy the same size as the original, intended to hang in a huge house like the one our cousins lived in, not in a farmhouse lobby. Dad made himself appear important by hanging his famous cousin in our hall. I wondered what effect it had, when friends like Melanie visited. She hardly had time to remove her coat before the man in the picture fixed her with a steely glare.

With a black, glazed background, almost indistinguishable from the sitter's clothes, its darkness was endless. Not one jot of colour, just patches of white on oceans of black. The collar and cuffs were the only parts to stand out against a soot-coloured necktie and velvet lapels. Maybe Edward Millais, the artist, thought that to be serious he must give up colour. I pictured his studio with rows of paint-pots of gold, mustard, primrose, burgundy, blues from forget-me-not to navy, and greens that glistened and gleamed in many shades, but the portrait hadn't a hint of them.

113

Reaching the bottom step as I ran down stairs, I had to stop myself from banging into the image of that man with his hands held in front of him, his thin lips, side-whiskers, sharp chin, and head of thinning hair. His eyes were forceful and determined, not warm or kindly or twinkly. I suspected he wouldn't have given me a second look. In turn, I felt no kinship with the Grand Old Man. He fuelled in me a longing to show two fingers to him, even blow a raspberry or two. Yet 'the women of England' paid the bill for the portrait, it said. His father was a trader and had tons of slaves, more than 2000 in the Americas, but he never met any and the Crown paid him almost a million pounds to give them up. I also learned on my own and in school that among the very first slaves on the plantations in the colonies were the Irish and Scotsmen: those the Republican, Cromwell, sent as his prisoners nearly 400 years ago.

Dad also hung a portrait of his own father in the passageway connecting the sitting, television, and dining rooms. At the end of the passage was a pencil sketch of Dad's Mum, Cecil, by an unknown French artist. If the family failed to push the boat out for her, they made an effort for Hugh, Dad's Dad, by commissioning a famous artist for him. When it was finished they hung it in the dining room at Kailzinet.

Dad hung the copy of his Dad's portrait near the sketch of his Mum, but close to a couple of pegs on which we shoved our coats. More often than not, a rainproof concealed the painting, or Lis' scarf obliterated her grandfather's nose, mouth and neck while my mack blotted out his right side, from the crown of his head to the hem of his jacket.

"Who's he?" I asked as I stretched up to yank down my jacket.

"Hugh, your grandfather," Dad answered.

I studied the man's moustache. "He looks like Hindenburg!"

"Hindenburg!" Dad was surprised. "How do you know that?"

"Mr Godfrey taught us."

"Tell me what you know about Hindenburg!" Dad was amused.

I found my school bag and in it, my history book, and reeled off the facts: "'Born in 1847, Prussian, from a landowning family;

the Kaiser's right hand, a wooden Titan!' I'll show you a photo".

"He's nothing like my father!" said Dad shoving the book aside. "He has a square head and his moustache is totally different!"

"All men had moustaches in the old days!" I said.

"Some had!" replied Dad. "Hindenburg's moustache is more flamboyant and...generous!"

I nodded. "His is like an upside-down fountain! Grand-dad's moustache is messier. Hitler's —"

"Hitler's? Dad was alarmed.

"His was really neat, like the black make-up brush Pat used when she was here!"

"Don't remind me of her!" Dad sighed.

Whenever I approached the coat pegs, next to Hugh's portrait, I'd study his face. I was still a baby when he died. Born in 1877, he was thirty years younger than Hindenburg and twelve years older than Hitler.

"Do you know something?" added Dad. "My Dad's moustache was halfway between the plutocratic extravagance of Hindenburg and the angular neatness of Hitler, that proletarian demagogue! They were all of a kind, above politics as they dominated them."

I saw the prism of Dad's hate. Boy, did he hate! He loathed. Often when he remembered his Dad, his broad shoulders shook and his hands made fists, not of a fighter but of a hungry baby. Dad's long fingers and broad palms were practical and creative often. I could imagine them on Turner. Dad won the top prize at Eton for drawing and painting, but his dad didn't let him go to art school. "No son of mine will be an artist!" he had said.

I stared again at the portrait of Hugh, done by James Gunn whose portraits were anything but daring or outré: a sober limner for a sober sitter. Only the spines of the books in the background have color. In a plain suit, Hugh sits in his library, that he created, but he's not smug. He looks sad and lacking in confidence. Maybe he was afraid of being middling, though he'd received plenty plaudits: a knighthood and fellowship to many societies, and praise for his book, a study of birds, said to be 'a little classic'.

The bird book used old illustrations by a Dumfries limner,

Thomas Watling. Afterwards, Hugh wrote a book about Watling, to get him more credit. It took Hugh five years of research and was printed in 1938. Dad didn't want to, but he showed it to me.

Watling was a scandal. Arrested and charged with forging Bank of Scotland notes, he was sentenced to a penal colony in Australia: On the way, in Cape Town, South Africa, he escaped from his ship the 'Daedalus', but was recaptured and sent on to the Antipodes.

In New South Wales, Watling was employed by John White, the author of 'A Journal of a Voyage to New South Wales, 1790', to paint 'the non-descript productions of the country'. White, however, snaffled Watling's water color drawings, yet two portfolios, one signed, ended up in the British Museum.

It seemed strange that Hugh, a man knighted for his public service, a stickler for the law, and the son of Steuart Gladstone, one-time governor of the Bank of England should champion this Dumfries forger. But he loved Dumfries and Dumfries-shire. Too bad Hugh didn't see the need to champion his own son when he wished to be a painter: Dad should have made the birds his subject, not landscapes.

Near the drawing of Cecil was an oil painting of Dad while in the RAF, from 1941. It's a study in blue, not a sunny blue but more of a lowering sky. Those were dark days. I recognised Dad from his cobalt eyes, large nose, and dark brown hair but the frame slices off his crown. Born the day after the Great War began, his upbringing was still Victorian, not of cloth caps, clackety boots and back-breaking, soul-killing labour but of gravel-raked drives, slow-baked puddings, colourful Christmases and smiling servants.

Family photographs also showed Dad in uniform, but in one picture in the garden at Kailzinet with his Mum and Dad, he looks poised for sacrifice, like Isaac in the bible. He's dressed for the fire, with a cocky, little cap perched at an angle on his head. His Dad knows better. His shoulders sag as he stares at his son. A fierce intensity etches his stiff upper lip. Dad's parents are letting him go like they've done since he was a boy, to school and university. They're letting him go into gunfire and hell; abandoning him to the skies.

116

Dad painted in oils before the war, and in water colors afterwards. He sketched the farm from every angle. It was picturesque, he said. The dairy and sheds looked out across the Moss of Cree towards Cairnsmore, a gentle hill. Close to the Irish Sea where the warm Gulf Stream flowed, the land never had deep snow. The Cree was a salmon river, fished with rod and fly on its upper reaches and, passing our farm it was wide, salty and tidal, with trap nets from boats. The river left the ground fertile with silt before it emptied into the Solway estuary.

Carsenestock was the second of seven farms you arrived at on the Moss of Cree when travelling from Newton Stewart. Each farmhouse stood close to its byre, boiler house, dairy and Dutch barn.

At the end of the road, on a small hill stood the stagnant county seat of Wigtown. A hub of life once, when decisions were made and the law upheld in its town hall, it soon lost out to the upstart harbour town of Stranraer. Earlier, Wigtown saw the Dominicans build a monastery and plant Cox's orange pippin apples. Much earlier, when men like St. Cuthbert, St. Aidan and St. Columba were the globe-trotting executives of the Dark Ages, St. Ninian arrived by paddle in a coracle, a small wicker-framed boat, at a nearby cove, to spread his good news.

The Wigtown houses, Dad told me, had once been the homes of the gentry, who came from moor and bog to rest in comfort for the winter, but these houses now looked tawdry, each door and window-trim painted a different colour: lilac, royal blue, crimson, acid green and butterscotch yellow.

For centuries the Moss of Cree was wilderness, a mass of soggy peat, but an improving earl reclaimed part of it and set Irish cattle on the remainder. Two hundred years ago, fields near the river were given over to turnip, barley and grazing. The earl imported stones to build breakwaters and dykes to stop the river bank breaking off when the Cree flooded during the high tides of the equinox. The hinterland, the real Moss of Cree, wouldn't be reformed, and remained water-logged, impassable.

Once, it was easier to get to Galloway by boat than road, but the road now sliced through our farm, marking rich ground from poor, creating two nation-states for us. It segregated clover and sedge from bracken and myrtle, as a wall between. From our kitchen window, we might see a bus, lorry or private car and, in the distance, those flat, miserable acres, never properly explored, but set aside for beast, curlew and lapwing. The road stole the river's ancient function of thoroughfare to and from the Moss of Cree. The narrow asphalt was the official boundary between the farm's affluent 'West', where the grass grew waist deep and succulent, while over the 'Wall' was another place, unyielding, poor and un-cared-for.

Dad let 'the beasts' fend for themselves up on the Moss. They weren't distinguished enough to be called 'cows'. Each morning he or his ploughman fed them bales of hay, food parcels from the rich land. They were Galloway crosses, hardy and sure-footed, bred and raised for their meat. Save for the whisper of a hoof on the tarmac or a sputter of dung falling from their hind legs, they were silent slaves. Not long after we settled in, my Dad sought ways to develop his eastern bloc, by filling in the potholes on the track and liming a field out in the sticks. The plowman's Stygian task was to go there in early summer to cut back the bracken. When Dad realized the effort was to no avail, and the land beyond redemption, he sold the ground to the Forestry Commission so they could plant it with their sorry little samples of sitka spruce.

At least Dad now was gentry.

I FORGOT TO MENTION earlier that when Mum took Janet to Dr Sampsons' surgery in Wigtown for her injuries, Dad fetched me from school in our forest-green pick-up van with its HAG 46 number-plate. Mum got plenty of laughs driving that van, but they weren't fair as she was only thirty-six then.

Within a fortnight, Mum and Dad held a cocktail party and after the guests left, we played in the television room. In a corner on the right of the window stood our spinet. To be correct, it was a square piano. E C-P, Mum's musical friend, explained why we were wrong to call it a spinet, but we did.

Everything with E C-P was a lesson. Whenever we went for a walk she'd pick a wild flower, like a buttercup, and on top of its ordinary name she'd tell us what it was in Latin: ranunculus acris.

"Harpsichords and spinets are sounded by a plucking motion," she said. "while pianos have hammers and if you look inside your instrument, you'll see them, standing side by side, like soldiers; one for each string and when you touch the key, a hammer hits the string and sounds a note." Dad refused to change his mind; it was a spinet and always would be. "Never mind what it is, it's lovely," E C-P said of our instrument. "You should be proud of it."

We were proud. Our 'spinet' had a lovely amber sheen and a line of inlay ran along the length of the lid an inch from its edge. No one knew if its lacquered wood was walnut, apple, pear or rose-wood, or all of those, but above the keys was a lighter shade of wood, maybe because the inside of the piano rarely saw the light. The seller's name, J. Watlen, from London's Leicester Place was in the center. If you cleared the piano surface of lamps, books and fruit bowls, lifted the lid and supported it on a strut, you could see its hammers and strings, much like the cogs and wheels behind the glass door of our carriage clock standing on the man-telpiece.

The creamy-yellow keys were like an old person's teeth, but someone had carved a cross on Middle C. Our spinet had been in Dad's family for ages. Maybe even at the time when Anne

Dashwood was alive. Did she carve it with a pair of scissors, or a hat pin, or a kitchen knife, even though she never would have visited the kitchen in her house? I'd have liked to see Anne Dashwood at the keys, caressing the ivories, her slippered feet on the pedals, now lost. Where they went is anyone's guess. At first nobody told me about the history of the spinet. It looked obviously odd next to the television and a modern radiogram.

"It's quite old!" Dad admitted.

"Who bought it?"

"My guess is Bob Gladstone, or son, Tom. I don't know if anyone in the family was particularly musical." In Dad's eyes, the Gladstone men who made pots of money were more important than their women who played the piano, embroidered cushion-covers and played drafts. Some had babies all the time and others were often ill.

"Bob was a Liverpool merchant and Tom expanded the business, so he could afford dozens of pianos. I'd say, they bought this one in 1820 for their home in Liverpool, and when Tom moved to Dumfriesshire he took it with him."

But who carved the cross on the key of Middle C? Really Anne Dashwood was too old to have done it and Catherine, Bob's wife died before they bought the piano. For all I knew, Tom had older sisters, the right age to play it. Perhaps their father bought it to help them cope with their mother's death in 1818. Tom's cousin was William Ewart, whose younger sister, Helen was a real rebel who drank a lot and took a drug called opium. Could she have cut that cross in spite of or while trying to teach herself blind-folded? When learning at school about Gladstone and his enemy, Disraeli, I liked to think that my direct connection with the GOM was that cross possibly made by his sister.

When I tried out my scales, I discovered the spinet had another problem: the A above middle C was silent. Maybe Helen could be blamed for that too? But Dad and his brother Jim could have thumped the note so hard that it stopped working or lifted the lid and hid a stash of lead soldiers on the strings, or when Dad was older, he might have hidden a bottle of gin inside the piano and its weight snapped the string.

"Why didn't they hire a piano-tuner to fix it?" I asked. Dad and I were sitting in the television room; he in his easy chair, his long legs outstretched and his feet resting on a footstool.

"He was too mean!" Dad explained, referring to Hugh, his Dad. "Mind you, he loved music hall songs." Dad rose and strode to the spinet. Lifting its lid, he picked out a tune with his index finger with the top digit missing. "If you were the only girl in the world," he sang with gusto, "and I was the only boy. Nothing else would matter in the world today. We'd go on loving in the same old way."

"How soppy! He didn't sing that?" I sneered.

Dad nodded. "He could be a sentimental old fool but most of the time he was the opposite."

"Why?"

"That's the way he was, a narcissist we call it now."

I had no words for this comment. "Is that someone who's vain?"

"In a sense! Sometimes he was great fun! He loved the sea and he often sang, "I do like to be beside the sea, I do like to walk along the prom, prom, prom, Hear the brass bands play, 'tiddle-e-pom-pom, pom."" Like his father, Dad loved singing this song, more so when it rose to a high point with those pom, pom poms.

"Is that why you kept the spinet? To sing that silly song!"

"I may have a good ear but I needed the spinet to help keep me in tune!"

"Don't be silly! It's no help at all. It's totally out of tune!"

"You'll have to put up with it; we can't afford a piano tuner."

Even with complicated chords, the spinet made a thin, reedy sound. It's tone was soft. No matter how hard you pressed the keys, it sounded polite and well-mannered. It was perfect for well-brought up ladies, the kind Dad wanted his girls to become one day. I'm not so sure Mum did. Aged eighteen, she exchanged one uniform for another: her school tunic for a suit of khaki and Sam Browne belt. She drove trucks at night and found her way on roads with no sign-posts. She even shot down an enemy aircraft.

When she wasn't looking I'd lift the spinet lid and lean it on a strut for it to look like the sail of a ship, as Robert Louis Stevenson in his Edinburgh bedroom compared his bed to a boat. Our spinet was a frigate, its plank of polished wood the sail, propelling us through a sea of melody.

But there were signs of wear and tear An ugly circle of scalded wood lay on the left side of the piano lid, like the scar tissue of a burn victim. Its shape and size looked as if it was made by a hot mug of coffee or tea, ruining one hundred and thirty years of polishing.

"In the old days etiquette took care of furniture," said Dad. "We drank from cups with saucers, never mugs, and protected tables with place mats."

"Who burned the spinet?"

"I suppose, someone used to Formica," he suggested, "a metal-topped table, or a laminated surface. Poor old spinet!"

Caressing the scalded wood, my father seemed to be consoling a dowager robbed of her jewels. "You've been well and truly mugged," he said.

Pleased with his pun, he stretched out again on his easy chair, and read the Court Circular page of The Times, which arrived from London a day late. "Of course," he said after he'd finished scanning the 'hatches, matches and dispatches', we could always get a French polisher."

"Not on your Nelly!" Mum said appalled. She'd come in to collect her mending basket, "No furniture in my house will have that done to it."

"I thought it might be rather nice," said Dad.

"That glossy finish is horrible. French polishing is for furniture in boarding houses and dentists' waiting rooms, not a house like ours with such lovely pieces."

"If you don't want French polishing, how about getting the spinet tuned?" I suggested.

Dad shook his head. "Any spare cash we have goes towards your education," he said.

But something got into Dad, then. The attack on the spinet sped him into action. It was a symbol of his past but still real. The portrait of William Ewart Gladstone in the hall was only a copy.

You could smell the spinet's antique wood. It crowned our family tree with its own special scent.

Dad started in to polish the spinet now and again. Wearing a navy apron with narrow white stripes, he set to with a duster and tin of costly furniture polish. Mum liked seeing him domesticated. The only other time he wore work-clothes, long white overalls over an old pair of trousers and shirt, was on the dairyman's week-end off when Dad himself did the milking. I never saw her in an apron. To do so was to collapse into a kind of womanhood she couldn't abide. Anyhow, Mum didn't need to wear an apron or overalls. To clean the house she had Mrs Sykes, who lived at the end of the Moss of Cree road; every other morning during the week, Mum or Dad fetched her in HAG 46 from her cottage, so she could vacuum our carpets, make our beds, and dust furniture. Dad didn't trust Mrs Sykes to polish the spinet as she only had the sight of one eye and the other was far from perfect.

After she slammed the vacuum cleaner into the legs of the spinet and then the claw feet of Mum's Jacobean bookcase, Dad had to clean. With his special furniture cream, he smeared the piano lid outside and in, and on its legs and music-rest also, and worked up a nice sheen. Dad's polishing was a ritual. After his older brother inherited Kailzinet, his boyhood home, Dad felt demoted. All he took with him on leaving was the spinet and a canteen of silver, each spoon and knife crested with the family coat of arms and its motto, 'fidelis et virtute' (faithful and true).

We had another keyboard instrument, every bit as dilapidated and dysfunctional as our spinet: a grand piano. We didn't need it. I wasn't a budding Glen Gould or Ashkenazy, but I wanted to learn to play and, as the spinet was no use, Mum asked Uncle Jock and Aunt Anne if the grand piano once standing in the hall at Largie Castle, her childhood home, was available. She doubted it, as much of her past was lost or destroyed. Largie was pulled down after the War, its furniture and books sold but, as it happened, not the grand piano; that was stored in the stables. It arrived at Carsenestock on a wet afternoon in a cattle float driven by Jim Cameron. Dad and Tony helped push the piano down the ramp until it rested on the asphalt, its casters sticking in dung left by the cows as they ambled down to the field after being milked. Too bulky to squeeze through the back door, the piano got pushed along the crazy paving garden path until it reached the greenhouse at the front of the house. Then Dad and Tony managed to manoeuvere our new instrument into the far corner of the sitting room.

We had no proper piano stool, but the first time I sat at the grand and cupped my hands to the keys, I realised something was wrong, but I persisted, especially when Mum was so pleased now. Yet, I could barely hear any sound. My teacher had taken a lot of trouble to show me how to play. I tried to press the keys gently, as she advised, but they were incredibly stiff. A simple scale hurt my fingers. It was like hitting concrete. No matter how hard I tried, my playing sounded stilted and unfluid.

"What's the matter, Mary?" Mum asked as I fled in tears.

"It won't play properly!" I wailed, feeling stupid and clumsy.

"Come on, Mary. You need to practise. You know the saying: A bad workman always blames his tools!" Mum chuckled.

She was wrong. It was the piano's fault. If any keyboard, however grand, and ours wasn't a Steinway, Blüthner, or Bechstein but a Collard & Collard from London, stood in a damp out-house or stables, un-played and uncared for, its keys would languish.

But never mind. From time to time, Mum and Dad held cocktail parties, 'pay-back time', they called them for having lunch or dinner in others' houses. This was when the spinet and grand piano came into their own as playthings for uninterested children. While the grand served as a bar for whiskeys and bloody Mary's, the spinet took a side-board role, for bottles of orange juice, bowls of crisps, and a spare silver tray, a wedding present to Dad from the tenants and employees of Kailzinet.

Guests drank cocktails like gin and tonics on empty stomachs, then grabbed canapés, Twiglets and cheese straws from the silver tray as it was passed around by me, Lis or Janet. I helped Mum make the cheese straws. "Always flour before you start," she taught me. Guests entered through the garden gate and walked the path until they reached the greenhouse, our front door. Often, people arrived at the back by Dad's office. He appointed Lis to stand in the hallway under the portrait of W E Gladstone. Here, arms out-stretched, she collected coats, furs, tweed jackets and sometimes a velvet cape. Inside the sitting room with its thick pile burgundy carpet, I waited at the grand piano, asking guests as they entered the room, what kind of drink they wished. Mrs Miller wanted a generous G and T, Dr Sampson, a small sherry and Alicia Green-law a tonic only. Was she on the wagon again? I'd heard at lunch-time Dad telling Mum that she'd recently been in the Crichton. The word struck terror in most minds. At school, in the play-ground, when anyone acted strangely, we pointed our fingers to the side of our heads and shouted, "You're for the Crichton."

Dad was in his element, as master of ceremonies; Mum was less so. In a dark blue shift of wild silk, she looked matronly but not glamorous. After helping with the drinks, I handed around the cheese straws.

"How you've grown!" trilled Mrs Miller. Her voice sounded shaky. Helen Drew, grabbing the longest straw from the plate, asked, "I hear they're thinking of sending you to school down South!" She meant a boarding school in England. Scotland, as far as this peculiar throng was concerned, was North Britain. I noticed Mum with Mr Longman, who owned a sawmill near Stranraer. Smiling as she talked, I could tell she quite liked him. He wasn't tall or handsome but he had a way about him; with a certain confidence, he knew he attracted women.

Dad liked ordering us around on these occasions. "Mary, go into the kitchen and fetch more tonic water, and Lis, a seat for Mrs Drew!"

It was as if we were in a movie and our guests were extras. In a corner, were three men: Mr. Matthews, the family lawyer, Mr Sangster, a retired accountant, and Mr. Anderson, a businessman. I offered them each a sausage on a stick but they were deep in conversation about title deeds and shares and didn't notice me. I turned towards a group of women instead.

"So, Mary!" Lady Pritchet had a disarming habit of mine-sweeping. Starting at the crown of the head, her eyes scanned my body until they reached my feet. Selecting a sausage, she bit into it daintily. "I hear you're going to school in Bristol!"

"Not until I'm ten in four years' time," I replied, beating a hasty retreat.

Like a flock of birds, the guests disappeared, leaving Mum and Dad too high on gin to bother to cook a proper meal. So, we remained in the sitting room, polishing off the sausages, cheese straws and canapés. These parties served as an investment for my parents for the following six months. It earned them invitations to engagement parties, weddings, Christmas dances, Hogmanay reels, even a christening or silver wedding celebration.

"If you don't bother to invite people, you can't expect to be asked back." Mum declared.

To be socially excluded was unthinkable.

E C-P was the only guest to stay behind. Mum was touched. "Bless you, Elizabeth!" Her friend had offered to help clear up.

When we finished tidying the sitting room, we moved to the other with the spinet. "It's such a lovely piece!" E C-P announced. "I'm glad you took the precaution of covering the lid with a good oil cloth, Esther," she said as she removed the silver tray and placed it on the trolley beside her. It's so nice you haven't vandalised it," said E C-P. "People eviscerate these pianos by getting everything taken out of them; just like when I had my hysterectomy. Then, horror of horrors, they use the gap as a drinks cabinet."

"Sacrilege!" Mum exclaimed.

"Absolutely!"

"I don't know," Dad interrupted. "Why not? Especially here in old Wiggers when every other person is an alcy!" he stepped to the table beside the piano where a whisky bottle and soda siphon stood. Pouring himself a large tumbler, he sat down drawing his long legs with pointed feet on to his footstool.

"Come on, David," Mum protested. "It's not as bad as that. And although I'm totally unmusical, I'd never throw out the keys and strings of our spinet. What a felony! We're not total Philistines, you know!"

That night, we children opened the spinet lid and banged out a tune or two. It was really only scampering with one finger up and down the white keys, then the black.

As Janet, climbed from a chair onto the spinet's right side, she slipped and fell on to the floor, clipping her head on the spinet leg. She screamed and screamed. Blood poured from the scar on her forehead. Mum burst into the room. Dad phoned the doctor. This time he sent his assistant, a female practitioner. Janet kicked her in the tummy, pulled her hair and wailed and wailed. But, somehow the doctor managed to sew up her forehead again. For a short period, at least until Janet's wound healed, Mum and Dad didn't let us into the television room. They didn't trust us not to climb on the spinet.

"Maybe we should make it into a drinks cabinet, after all," said Dad.

"GIVE HIM MORE!"

"He's finished his bottle!"

"It's not enough."

"They told me he shouldn't have more until his next feed!"

"Don't listen to them! He's hungry! Can't you see?"

Remembering when, as a child, she over-fed her puppy and killed it, Mum dared not over-ride the nurse's instructions on how much to feed us as babies. While she obeyed rules to the letter of the law, Dad broke them. From the beginning, food was a source of conflict. For Dad, quantity was an important factor and he'd tell us about the day when, aged five, he stole a stilton cheese, from the Kailzinet dining room and hid in the garden under a bush to scoff it. Older sister Jean was no less greedy. To kid fellow diners into believing she was a moderate eater, after snatching plums from a bowl on the dining table, she hid all but three of the stones under her place mat.

Dad relied on Mum to rein in his appetite, not only for food, but for Italian opera, French impressionists, fast driving, and also daring feats in airplanes when he was younger. William Blake summed up his thinking: 'the road of excess leads to the palace of wisdom.'

Meal-times were a jousting arena, especially Sunday lunch. Dad had watched Zorro on television and fancied himself to be Douglas Fairbanks, minus the Spanish cape, sombrero hat and mask. Impersonating the Mexican Robin Hood, brandishing his sword, Dad made the carving of the joint into a Sunday ritual.

While Mum, in the kitchen, drained the peas or broccoli, Dad boldly carried the joint to the dining room hot-plate. Then, swish, swish, swish, as he swept the sharpener along the edge of the knife blade. "Are you hungry, Mary?" he asked.

Yorkshire pudding was Mum's hardest Sunday task, harder than getting ready for church, ensuring her beret-type turban sat straight on her bouncy, permed hair. Dad, whose demands were exacting, insisted on perfect Yorkshire pudding. As a boy he lived in five star luxury at Kailzinet, a mini kingdom. Gardeners grew produce and farmers raised cattle and sheep for them, housemaids cleaned, a butler served, and a chauffeur drove them around in the family car with Hugh's crest on the front passenger door. It had to be a Ford. Being high in the roof, it allowed my grandfather to wear his bowler hat while riding inside.

"Mind you do the Yorkshire pudding so it rises nicely, Esther!" At each attempt, Mum feared the outcome. Would the puddings turn out rock hard or soft and flabby? .

I didn't mind meat but I hated fat. "Try it! You don't know until you taste it," said Dad. So I did and spat it out. It was disgusting.

"You're not a Mrs Spratt, are you?"

"Who's that?"

"'Jack Spratt could eat no fat, his wife could eat no lean, so, between them both, they licked the platter clean.' That's the rhyme."

It fit Mum and Dad, but it was Dad who ate the fat and Mum, the lean. Her eating habits were experimental, while Dad's were conservative. He believed in a set way to cook everything from scones to salmon, preferring traditional fare. Meat and two veg with no garlic or herbs, and before the war at dinner, four, five or even six courses: melon and ground ginger, soup, after which came a fish dish, then a main course of pheasant or grouse, then pudding and a savoury or cheese to finish the meal. They ate off silver and porcelain, using freshly-laundered napkins. After all, Kailzinet had laundry maids and hot water by the bucket-load.

After the war, Dad found a slimmed-down life hard. But he knew what to wear, and understood wines and what to eat with a Reisling or Burgundy, and so expected Mum to cook posh.

In her new role, she consulted Constance Spry, discarding Mrs Beaton who wrote for grand mansions, advising cooks to use 'three pints of cream' in their recipes.

When my parents married, aunts and uncles gave them table cloths, which Mum never used as she had no laundry maids and a set of Worcester bone china and strangely-shaped aluminim saucepans. "I've got these square saucepans!" she announced to Dora one morning.

"You'll be telling me next you've got a round TV and toaster."

We did have circular tables, half-moon chairs and Colin once found a circular book in his Christmas stocking.

"The pans were a wedding present from Uncle Lewis!" Mum explained. Mum's four uncles were her mother's brothers. We weren't very interested in them as children. One was killed in World War 1, another had epilepsy, a third shot himself in Dublin, and the fourth, Lewis Crabbe, was a rear-admiral. Not wishing to boast, Mum failed to tell me that while in China, Lewis had been a bit of a hero in saving a ship from the Japanese on the Yangtze, one of the longest rivers in the world. But I found out from Dad.

Dad gave me a history lesson about China. "Terrible mess, you know. Warlords all over the place. And the Japs waiting in the wings to seize the pickings. Then, the Communists took over. What a mess!"

Chinese names were a nightmare to spell. So was Timbuktoo. Going to Timbuktoo was different from being sent to Coventry. One was wandering aimlessly at your own leisure, the other was without choice.

Mum never knew why her uncle didn't realise how difficult those saucepans were to wash. "Food always gets caught in those corners," she complained.

"He never had to do the dishes," said Dora.

Come to think of it, Great Uncle Lewis was like Granny's friend Dorothea, wife of the Chief of Police in Cairo who, never having done her dishes before, would wash each plate, cup and saucer under a tap of hot, running water, instead of in a big bucket.

"She didny run the water into a bowl?" Dora was incredulous. Mum shook her head. "So wasteful!"

Dora had met Dorothea Russell. So had I. I didn't like her. In Granny's pantry, she taught me how to make butter pats with a tool that curled butter into whirls. "Press gently!" she ordered. "Not so hard!" She snatched the tool from my hand to show me. I tried again. "That's no good, child! Give it back to me!"

One day, instead of porridge or cornflakes at breakfast, Mum gave us muesli. Soaking oats in water over-night, she added the next morning cashews, apple chunks, bananas and raisins."

"What's that? Pigs' swill?" Dad suggested.

"Shut up, David! It's muesli. Something we had before the war when I went on that cruise with Mother. It's healthy. Raw oats, fruit and nuts are excellent for one's insides."

"Gut-rotting, I'd say! What's wrong with porridge, bacon and eggs, toast, butter and marmalade? They call it 'a full English' in roadside caffs!"

"Don't for heaven's sake tell Dora; she hates anything English. Anyway, we're Scottish but for breakfast, I'd prefer to eat Swiss, thank you very much!"

Dad did love to experiment but with speed, new appliances and labour-saving devices. He was the first farmer on the Moss of Cree to modernise his byre by investing in a milking parlour. In 1953, he bought a television for the Queen's coronation. A little later, he bought a soda stream for making lemonade and fizzy water. Then a dishwasher and even a tape recorder.

Mum recoiled from making egg custard. It was her pet hate. It always curdled. She'd stand in front of the cooker on the cold, tiled floor in the kitchen. The room had doors and stairs leading everywhere. "I feel I'm in Piccadilly Circus," Mum moaned.

"I've a marvellous new pudding, Esther! It takes five minutes to make. It says so on the back of the packet." Dad was keen to show Mum how swift he could be. In his boast on rustling up quick desserts, Dad was throwing down the gauntlet, Ready-made meals were beyond the pale for Mum.

"I found it in the Co-op!" he said. "It's called Dream Topping. It's a cross between custard and cream. It's very nice."

"Dream Topping?" Mum was scathing.

"I said it was very nice!" Dad protested pouring the powder from the packet into a bowl and adding milk. Within seconds the mixture had thickened.

"How could you, David? We live on a dairy farm and have pure cream. When it's artificial, food factories call it crème. They spell it the French way if it's counterfeit!"

When it came to beef, Dad made a fuss if it wasn't local and of prime quality. He bought our meat himself from Logan, the butcher, opposite the cattle market in Newton Stewart, and each summer the net fishermen, who crossed our field to reach their fishing beat on the river, presented us with a salmon.

Cautious in the kitchen, Mum cooked by the book, not cutting corners. Dad liked French words, but not their food. Bouillabaisse was bad but 'hors d'oeuvre' was okay. His favourite phrase was 'un embaras de richesse' as not only a Victoria sponge, but also a walnut and chocolate cake appeared on the tea table. He loved to see mounds of baking. When frivolous he'd utter 'je ne sais quoi' and call some people naive or effête. He knew plenty in Wigtownshire, in their decaying mansions. To him, 'chi-chi', meant over-dressed or citified. Another of Dad's words was 'rapprochement', something often needed with difficult people.

"Garlic! Oh, my goodness, no!" he said. Eating garlic was like wearing a tie pin or a gold medallion; only exhibitionists did that.

In light of all his Gallicisms, Mum began to cook French. To help her, Granny lent us a book, 'Tante Marie's Kitchen', translated into English by Charlotte Turgeon, and Mum found the correct ingredients though the only shop in Newton Stewart that sold olive oil was the chemist, in a miniscule bottle, for softening dry skin. And in Scotland, truffles were chocolate delicacies, not fungi dug up by specially trained pigs. Then too, Dad wouldn't countenance fresh-water fish like pike, perch or eel.

Consulting Tante Marie, Mum tried serving us 'boeuf bouilli'.

"What's this?" asked Dad. "Boiled beef? How could you? You ruined it. Whoever thought of that?"

"The French!"

"They would!" Then, very unexpectedly, Dad rose from the table and skipped around the hot-plate singing, "Boiled beef and carrots, boiled beef and..."

Mum didn't approve of all Tante Marie's recipes. "Who'd want to eat frogs' legs or snails?"

"I don't know," argued Dad. "Prawns are just cockroaches!"

"OK, David!" Mum was irritated. "But I draw the line on veal."

Tante Marie didn't mention horse-meat in her book, but she had recipes for outlandish animal parts, and Mum knew it would be a losing battle if she served us fried beef brains, tripe Lyonnaise, whatever that was, and larded sweetbreads, or calf's head with French dressing or calf's feet on blanquettes. Mum finally gave up on cuisine française but the book came in handy for helping her make the odd paté, pastry and roux sauce. Dad won in the end. He usually did.

When it came to food, Granny influenced us. She never stayed during Lent; as carrying out her obligations was too difficult then. At home, she kept silence for two hours each morning, prayed for an hour in the afternoon and stopped spreading marmalade on her toast at breakfast-time. That was her greatest sacrifice.

"Why marmalade, Granny?"

Of all sacrifices, forgoing marmalade gave her most pain except perhaps for the dentist. She expressed terror at the prospect of a visit. Lis and I argued about which was the least nasty: the high-pitched screaming drill or the low-sounding, growling one.

In the playground we asked each other what we'd 'give up' and which would we choose: to be blind or deaf, an arm or leg, a Mum or a Dad. I wasn't sure. Could I give up ice creams? I preferred not to. I polished them off quickly. Lis finished hers first, then me and lastly, Janet. She always hoarded her chocolate and sweets, Mars Bars, Bounty's, Fry's Chocolate bars and Smarties, stashing them in a drawer in her room.

When food was plentiful, with oranges, peaches and grapes from Southern Africa and lamb and butter from New Zealand, we entered a bountiful period. Granny tried to control our hearty appetites. "Don't gobble, Mary!" she warned. "After a meal, you should get up from the table feeling satisfied but not full."

After lunch we lined up in front of her to receive our sweets. She kept them in a tin, painted cyclamen pink. "One chocolate for you, Mary! No! One! Not two! And a boiled sweet. A barley sugar. I don't care if you don't like it, you're having it. All of you. And a toffee and a piece of fudge or tablet as you call it here. That'll do. You don't want another visit to the dentist, do you?

Granny may not have approved of our greed at meal-times but

she couldn't abide faddy eaters. People should eat what was put in front of them, no matter what. Even disgusting milk puddings like junket. Our greed was manageable when the family ate alone but not so good when guests came for dinner. So, before anyone arrived, Mum read us the riot act: "Remember, it's FHB!"

"What's that?"

"Family hold back!"

This was achievable except when overly slow eaters visited. Uncle Jim, Dad's younger brother, was the worst. Unusually, Mum and Dad pushed their last mouthful of food around their plate in the hope of not finishing before Uncle Jim. The rest of us didn't wait.

— THE UNHARMIOUS BLACKSMITH —

HIS CAP WAS FILTHY and his face dripped with sweat but we loved visiting him. We wouldn't miss it for the world. Usually, Mum drove to his cottage to fetch him so he could shoe our ponies at home. The forge stood by the river opposite his house and the yard was full of scrap metal: old harrows, ploughs and iron gates. Inside the smiddy was the fire and on a table perched the craw, a crow. "Get the hell oot," he yelled at the bird, slapping with his cap at its feathers. "Awa' with you! You black bugger!"

Mum chuckled, wondering which looked the blackest: Gus or his crow. He had no phone so our visit was to find out when he would come to shoe Marty, my pony, and Patsy, Lis's, which she shared with Janet .

"You've got their correct size, haven't you, Gus?" Mum asked.

"Aye, Mrs! I've got the measurements. That's the big pony and the wee yin!"

"So, how are you, Gus?" asked Mum.

He leant against the table groaning under the weight of horse-shoes, hammers and other tools.

"No bad, Mrs. A wee bit back pain. A Clydesdale kicked me a year back, a bloody great lump of a thing, down at the farm in Sorbie. They still dae the ploughing with the horses there, and he damaged my kidney, or so the doctor said. Oh, aye, I'm fair tired now," he sat down on a broken back chair and wiped his forehead with his cap. "The doctor says it's the right one. "

"Oh, dear, Gus, I'm so sorry."

When we returned two days later in order to drive him to Carsenestock, he was in fine fettle.

"Oh, Mrs!" his voice was like a purr, soft and eager when he talked about fishing and poaching. The road was narrow and twisting, and as Mum yanked the steering wheel from right to left, she egged him on, keen to listen to one of his wild stories. "What did you do this time, Gus?" He was known for stalking the river below his house and tickling fish; usually trout but some-times he trapped salmon when it leapt upriver.

"I was doon," he pointed where he had been with a nod of his head, "at the water, waiting for the fish to swim up to the rock. There's a ledge there they shelter under. I hunkered doon on my belly on the bank and saw one, its tail moving. So I knelt on my right knee and lowered my hand in the water and pushed my fingers under the rock and touched its tail. And wi my forefinger, drew my hand along its belly towards the head, under the gills. You ken if you do that, it puts the trout into a sleep. You catch it quickly, flip it oot the water, give it a dunt on the head and it lands in your pocket. Do ye ken, Mrs? They call it guddling."

"Oh, Gus," said Mum in mock shock, "the things you get up to with your guddling!"

"You dinny ken the half of it, Mrs!" He lifted his cap, scratched his almost bald head, and replaced it.

"I mind when I guddled six salmon on that river, in one day."

"Six? You're exaggerating!" Mum was nobody's fool.

"Do ye ken how I got them back home undetected?"

"I can't imagine how?"

Gus looked coy. He removed his cap again and said, "Och, I willny tell you. No, I willny!"

It was tantalising not to know.

Not long afterwards, Mum summoned Paddy McDonald and his float. He drove cattle and sheep to market. He also transported ponies to Pony Club meetings, horse events like gymkhanas and hunter trials. This time, he arrived at Carsenestock to drive Marty and Patsy to a three day event at Duntulm, not far from Gus' smiddy. I climbed up to sit in the lorry next to Paddy who was driving. The first day was a show-jumping contest, the second, a cross-country course consisting of ditches, dyke walls and wooden fences that horse and rider must tackle. The third was dressage. I was to compete on the first day only, when, riding on Marty, I'd have to negotiate a course of obstacles painted red and white and positioned in a confined space.

On our way, we passed Gus' house and turned the corner by the river. Ahead was a woman pushing a pram, its hood raised, but as Paddy slowed down to a snail's pace to overtake it safely, we peeked at what was inside. Expecting a baby sleeping, we were surprised to see instead a large fish tail lying on the pillow and at the foot, coming out of the blanket, a large fish eye in a fish's head. The woman wore a cloche hat on her head, but her face showed a clear five o'clock shadow. Too small for the woman's head, her hat lay askew, revealing a bald patch on the crown. "Hey, that's no wumman!" Paddy said. "That's Gus Campbell!" He slammed his foot on the brake, stopped the vehicle and leapt out. "Hey, there Gus! What you doing in they clothes, fancy yerself a woman now?"

"Get away wi' you!"

"Needs must when the devil drives? Oh, I see!" Paddy peered into the pram. "Nice wee wean you've got there. I'll no be givin it a kiss, mind! Oh, you've two o' them. Twins, then?"

Paddy lifted the coverlet to reveal three more salmon lying across the other two.

"Quintuplets! Your poor Mrs! She's had a rough time!"

"Stop your blethering, man," Gus was not at all amused by Paddy's banter, "An' give me a hand."

"Och, I can see yer pram's weighted doon. Watch you dinny break its axle. You dinny want yer weans tumbling on to the ground."

"For Chrissake, can you no give me a hand? Give me a ride in yer lorry. Come on, man!"

Paddy wasn't so sure. "I don't want bother from the Police," he said. "I've seen them up the road."

Gus shuddered. "Help, then,"

Paddy agreed. He moved to the back of the float, opened the door that lowered as a ramp for animals to climb in and out, and ordered Gus to push his pram up in to the vehicle. "Mind you don't frighten the horses with your quintuplets!" he warned.

"You're no leaving me in here wi' they ponies. I ken they two. That wee yin's a bad-tempered besom."

"What's up wi' you, Gus? Feart they'll eat yer weans? They're no flesh-eaters, they ponies."

Paddy relented and Gus came and sat next to us in the front.

When we arrived at Duntulm, Gus disappeared; we didn't set

eyes on him again during the event. I was preoccupied anyway with our performance in the show-jumping competition, when I hoped against hope to manage a clear round on Marty. We did clear all fences but at the five-barred gate, she stalled and refused to jump. I turned her around, urging her once more to clear the fence and this time she succeeded, but we were penalised with three faults and came in third.

Back home, on the morning following the event, Dad looked out the back door to find, lying on the dusty door-mat, an object wrapped in a piece of old sacking. He opened it up to discover a salmon. Evidently one of Gus' wee-yins.

WE HAD A YOUNG driver and an old one. At 3.15 pm one or the other drove the bus to the school gate. We waited in a huddle for it to arrive. On this occasion, the old man came. First on the bus was Melanie Fraser, then me. Twelve others followed to take up their seats. First off, at Nether Barr, were the twins, who were very clever, cleverer than Bobby Strang, the policeman's son who was clever too; then Fiona at Upper Barr. Shortly afterwards, the bus turned left to Lamachan View where Melanie descended with the Landers boys and Johnny Black. At Carty Tile Works, Tommy Wilson got off; he always had a tear in his trousers, a whine in his voice and was awfully small for his six years. I was the last to leave the bus; that was if Angela from Polwhilly cottage wasn't there.

The next stop was our road-end, after the rushes surrounding the bog, where Lis, Melanie and I had created our garden and seen our first adder. Dad's friend, Enoch, whose name reminded me of a railway station, sneered at us on hearing our story. Like many of my parents' friends, he disliked children and said our reaction to the snake was very Freudian. "What does that mean?" I asked Dad. He and Mum met my question with silence: I'd touched another taboo.

This day, the bus driver drove straight past our road-end and passing the big field by Kelly port, stopped the bus. Instructing me to stand beside him as he sat in the driver's seat, he fondled my right leg. Then we sailed past Polwhilly and the Grange of Cree, where he turned the bus round and drove back down the road to Carsenestock to deposit me. This happened four or five time before anyone else knew. Then the older man left, and the young driver took over. At our road-side, I caught the furious look on his face. His rage reminded me of what Mum sometimes said when one of us was angry, 'if looks could kill!'

After the old bus driver got the sack, the story of his wrong-doings went the rounds of the cattle market. At the Thursday tup sales, when farmers leant over the rail in the ring, nodding their bid to the auctioneer and congregating later for a whisky in the George, they talked. "What? Dougie? What did he dae?"

They found out that he'd been driving the school bus with one hand and stroking the legs of school-girls with the other.

"Why isn't the old man driving us to school any longer?" asked Lis. Mum was whisking egg whites for a cheese soufflé. "Go and lay the table, darling," she replied. "and let me get on with this. If you don't whisk the eggs properly, the soufflé doesn't rise! You've no idea how difficult this is."

Because nobody discussed these events with me, I saw them as a jigsaw puzzle with missing pieces. In a way, Mum and Dad encouraged me to doubt it ever happened. I was left feeling I had done something wrong. Yes, I was a bad girl or, if not bad, not quite right.

Soon after the incident, Mum got appointed secretary of the Wigtownshire branch of The League of Pity, the junior branch of the Scottish Society for the Protection of Children. Young people on the lucky side of the social divide raised funds for those who were not. For our first meeting, Mum drove us to a large house on the outskirts of Newton Stewart, where a group of children came to listen to my mother explain how fortunate we were.

"Some girls and boys," Mum announced, "never have a proper bed-time and their Mummy's only give them crisps and lemon-ade for supper." It crossed my mind that Mum's descriptions of deprivation weren't so bad, after all.

Later, she warned me, "If a man offers you a sweety, refuse!" Soon afterwards, Mum went on holiday in the Western Isles with her friend, Margaret Mackenzie while we were dispatched to an assortment of relatives. Janet and I stayed with Aunt Caitriona or Cassy, but we weren't allowed to call her that. She was married to Simon, my Mum's older brother. They lived in an old shooting lodge on the Lee and Carnwath estate near West Linton, now an Edinburgh dormitory town. So, another long car journey had to be made. Mum did her best to amuse us along the way. As we neared Lanarkshire, she warned us that the road would change colour.

"What colour, Mummy?" asked Janet.

"Guess!"

"White?"

"No!"

"Blue!"

"No!"

"Green? " We kept guessing til we mentioned pink.

"That's it!"

"Why, Mummy?"

"The stone's pink because it comes out of the quarry that way!"

Kailzinet was built in pink stone too.

Janet and I didn't want to stay with Aunt Caitriona, as her sons, Angus and Hamish were away. Sue, five years older than me, was at boarding school. Norman was there, but he was just two so he didn't count. Aunt Caitriona tried to make us feel welcome but she didn't have much of a way with children, except she saddled up a small pony and took us both for rides. Because it was unusually hot that year, we paddled in a nearby river.

Aunt Caitriona's kitchen was a sight. She had all the new gadgets, fitted kitchen cabinets, and a breakfast bar, which was the last word in transatlantic sophistication. In the fridge, standing in front on the middle shelf, was a large bottle containing cream, as thick as toffee, like I'd never seen.

"How come their cream is so thick?" I asked myself. When I asked aloud, my aunt told us they kept a Jersey cow to supply milk exclusively for them. Ours was no thicker than the top of the milk and we were forbidden to take it anyway:

"I can't take any from the dairy," Dad had admitted. "If the creamery caught us, that'd be it!"

Towards the end of our stay, Sue returned home but wouldn't talk to anyone. I surprised myself by being the chatty one. Not many of my older cousins spoke to me, except for Aunt Jean's youngest daughter, Davina. On the whole, seniority in our family meant the cold-shouldering of younger relatives. I shrugged my shoulders and promised myself that one day I would be an older cousin and cold-shoulder juniors to my heart's content.

BECAUSE OF WHAT HAPPENED on the school bus, Mum and Dad moved Lis and Janet from Penninghame School to Hartfield in Ayr, a weekly boarding school whose sandstone building was near the old racecourse. As for me, I wasn't to remain at Penninghame either. Like Mum and Dad before me, I was destined for a proper boarding school 'down south' and in Primary 5, I sat the entrance exam for it. Melanie couldn't understand why I had to go so far away. "Why all the way to England?" she asked. We stood by the front door of the big school where each classroom window was set so high that pupils only saw the sky when they looked out.

"My Mum and Dad went to boarding school in England," I told her as I leant my foot on the boot-scraper, used by people with muddy foot-wear. "We don't want mucky shoes in this class, do we?" Mrs Trotter, our class teacher had warned..

"Why?" asked Melanie.

"I don't know. That's the way it was. It still is," I shrugged my shoulders.

She wasn't convinced. "My Mum wouldn't send me away to a boarding school! She'd miss me!"

I hadn't considered why mine wished to. It was like gutting fish, plucking dead pheasants or beating dogs for chasing sheep; unpleasant but it had to be done. After all, not everything was nice in this world. I disagreed with Melanie who thought it unnatural to send a child away to school. Her father, she told me, thought it was snobbery that got my parents to do it. I didn't want to tell her that I felt sorry for her staying at home and attending the Douglas Ewart High School after she left Penninghame. What influenced my opinion were the novels I'd read about boarding schools where girls with glossy hair in pony tails, had midnight feasts in the dorms and at holiday-time, rode ponies in gymkhanas and won rosettes, which they pinned on the wall of their bedrooms. So, I saw deprivation of this kind as a form of privilege. Heartache and tears went with exclusivity. All my cousins went to boarding school and in time, so would Lis, Janet and Colin.

Dora was concerned too. When she saw my choice of color for the name tapes, which were to be sewn on to each garment of my school uniform, she asked, "Whit are you doing? Yellow? Oh, my! What a color! It's the devil to read, is it no? You'll need yer spectacles for that. Why not red, green or navy, for goodness sake? Not yellow! Yellow's for the sun or for gold. Not for sewing on your name to your jumper."

I insisted on yellow. I wanted my clothes to remind me of home when I was far away. Yellow was for the sun over the hill, my hill, the one where the German pilot came to grief and the Duchess lived. Yellow was for crocuses and daffodils in the garden and the buttercups in the fields. If we found one, we held the flower beneath our chins, asking each other if we liked butter. We found celandines growing by the ditches and marsh marigolds and irises in the water. All were yellow. At the beach, the sand was yellow, a dusky beige-yellow but yellow nonetheless. Gold is yellow too, I said to Dad.

"Very vulgar!" he replied. The idea of wearing gold other than a signet ring or pocket watch was out of the question. He stuck to silver.

"Oh, aye," said Dora. "I mind when every cloud had a silver lining. No now! All my clouds are black, or grey." She looked out of the window. "See them?" She pointed to a puffy array of sultry grey in the sky. My fondness for yellow extended to birds: yellow hammers and canaries. And to garden plants like winter jasmine and mimosa. To satisfy my craze for the color, Mum bought two skeins of double knitting wool in primrose yellow and knitted me a pullover.

Like Melanie, my other class-mates in Primary 5 didn't understand why I was leaving Penninghame for another school hundreds of miles away. I didn't really understand either but it seemed normal. Mum had gone to one herself when her nanny had tied a label around her wrist and packed her off on the steamer to Glasgow. I was luckier, at least for my interview at the school. With Mum accompanying me, I was to take the Paddy, the night train, to London's Euston station. At Paddington, we

143

caught a train to Bristol; our destination was Badminton School, near the edge of the Downs.

At 11 pm, on time the train arrived at the platform of Newton Stewart station. Mum clutched a small case and Dad carried another into our compartment. We hadn't booked a sleeper. Lis had had whooping cough, which prevented us from knowing when we could leave until Dr Sampson told us we could that evening. In our compartment was a man who stretched himself out on all the seats of one side. Mum told me to lie down on the other. I'd just dozed off when she tapped me on the shoulder. "We're going into the next compartment. Quick! Put on your shoes and follow me."

"Why?" I asked, brushing sleep off my eyes.

"Never mind!" she snapped. In our new compartment was a Northern Irish family with three children. The mother offered Mum a cup of coffee from her thermos flask and handed me a Penguin biscuit. After I'd finished eating it, I pretended to sleep.

"That's an odd one next door!" I heard Mum tell the woman, marvelling at the way her voice changed whenever she talked to different people. "It was being in the FANY's that did it," she'd explain when challenged about the different accents she assumed often : they were Scots, Glaswegian, Cockney and West Highland. "We met all types there!" she had told me while plucking a brace of pheasants shot by Dad at Uncle John's shoot. Mum exulted in her role of farmer's wife, not the mate of a hobbyist but a real one. "I'm not the wife of a gentleman farmer," she would say proudly. And she wasn't. She knew more about Dad's beef cattle than he did; when to take them off a section of grazing and when to send them to market.

The woman offered Mum a cigarette. She hesitated and then accepted and let the woman light it with her gas lighter. "I didn't like the way he looked," Mum said, folding her right leg over the left and leaning back against the compartment seat. Smoke furled upwards, concealing a picture under the luggage rack, of St. Ives in Cornwall.

"You get all sorts off the boat," said the Irish woman. "I mind once there were a few that I could swear were Provos. Can't be sure," she sniffed and leant back. "You a Protestant?" she asked.

Mum was taken aback. "Yes, I suppose. Not Catholic, anyway."

"I could tell. You can always tell a left-footer from a right."

At Euston station, we encountered crowds, a loud-speaker, the ticket barrier, and porters with luggage-laden trolleys. "Keep close," Mum warned. We were over-nighting in a town called Sevenoaks. Why not Five Ash, I asked myself, or Three Cedars, Ten Spruce or Six Chestnuts but it was Seven-oaks in Kent. There were no Gaelic-sounding names here. If you dug the soil, you found chalk not peat. Even the plants and trees were different. "You get plenty cherries here. During the war we got sick of the taste of them, we had so many," Mum told me.

We stayed overnight with Margaret Spicer, Mum's old school friend and her mother, who owned a dog called Puck. He could offer you his paw, jump through a hoop and even nudge shut an open door. In glorious denial, I hadn't yet envisaged how it would be when I went to boarding school. The following day we left for Bristol and on our arrival, I heard a voice announcing "Bristol, Temple Meads". It was late. We hadn't booked a hotel. There was too little time to do so before leaving home. On hailing a taxi, the driver warned us that the city was very busy. Bristol Rovers Football Club was playing a home match and most hotels were booked up. He drove us to one, but found no room there, then another, and another. "The only hotel I can think of is the Shangri-La, down by the docks," said the driver. "I don't recommend it but 'needs must when the devil drives'.

On entering reception with its dim lighting, we stepped on to a soft piled carpet and heard a door bang at the end of a passage-way. A woman's shrill laughter thinly veiled a leering man's voice.

"Number 10, two floors up," said the receptionist to us. Mum slept little that night. "I couldn't manage it," she announced the following morning. "Too much coming and going, I'm afraid."

Passing the Downs, a large, open space of grass where people strolled and walked their dogs, we arrived at the school gate. Beyond it was the games field and a modern building, followed by another, not so modern. We ended up at a Victorian mansion, which housed the head-mistress' study. A secretary approached and ordered us to sit at a table, its surface covered in newspapers.

"What should I say to this lady?" I asked.

"Just be yourself!" Mum advised.

That wasn't so easy, I sensed, I didn't know who I was.

"Talk about the books you read, the walks you do. Anything! Maybe even about Marty!"

A door opened and a tall woman with white hair emerged.

"Esther!" she exclaimed. Mum had warned me that the head-mistress had once taught her. "How lovely to see you." She stared down at me, " So, this is Mary! Come in!"

Her room was different from the rest of the school. The floor was thickly carpeted and it had comfortable armchairs. "Sit down, Mary!" she said. She placed herself in a swivel chair by her desk and faced me. "What is your favourite book?" she asked. I knew she'd approve of Kenneth Grahame's 'The Wind in the Willows', Charles Dickens' 'A Christmas Carol' and Frances Hodgson Burnett's 'The Secret Garden'. The one I preferred was 'Brendan Chase' by Balfour Browne.

"Why is that your favorite?" I told her, that it was about two brothers who ran away from home because they didn't want to go to boarding school. They went to live inside the trunk of a hollow tree in the woods and fished for food in a lake and picked berries to eat. "Is that what you want to do, Mary?" she asked with a smile.

I realised then what I had said and wondered if I'd ruined my chances of being accepted into the school. Did I really care? This wasn't a particularly nice place. It might be better to enter Primary 6 at Penninghame and be with Melanie and my other friends. But Mum had decided, especially after that incident with the bus driver.

Having recovered from whooping cough, Lis welcomed us back home. Not long afterwards, I discovered I had a rash all over my body. Dr Sampson said it was a spring rash and handed me an ointment. Summer came and the rash remained. Then autumn arrived, and this time when I entered the surgery, Dr Samspon expressed bemusement. He decided to send me to a skin specialist in Dumfries, which alarmed Mum. As soon as I entered his room and sat down, the doctor asked to see my hands. With a scalpel, he pierced the skin between my thumb and forefinger and extracted the offending body. A kind of bug, like a midge had burrowed under my skin, causing the rash. The specialist gave Mum a large bottle of white lotion. It looked like distemper used for painting walls. Back home, Mum painted me all over. It was torture. I felt as if I'd been stung by hundreds of wasps.

It was fit punishment for having contracted scabies, I supposed, presumably from having slept in the dirty hotel in Bristol.

The city as Dad saw it

— Clothes List —

Badminton School Winter Term 1958

1 tweed overcoat
1 felt hat / scarf
2 prs gloves
1 gaberdine raincoat
1 blazer
2 tweed skirts / 2 tunics
5 blouses
1 cardigan
1 jumper
1 pair games shorts
4 aertex shirts
4 pairs games socks
1 hooded games sweater
1 pair plimsolls
1 pair hockey/lacrosse boots
6 pairs socks
4 vests
6 pairs white pants
3 pairs navy pants
24 handkerchiefs
2 pairs pyjamas/nighties
1 bed jacket
1 dressing gown
2 pairs lace-up shoes
1 pair indoor shoes
1 pair wellingtons
1 pair slippers
2 laundry bags
1 toiletry bag
a shoe cleaning outfit

This was my introduction into uniforms and uniformity, in what I wore and in attitude. At the foot of the list was the outfitter's name and address: Daniel Neal, Portman Square, London.

Aligning itself with other English private schools, the shop's list was bamboozling but Mum checked it carefully and ordered my uniform. Apart from the latter, I was allowed to wear mufti, my own clothes, so long as skirts and dresses weren't too long or short, the toes of my shoes not too pointed, the heels no higher than an inch and tops, blouses and jumpers adequately covered my breasts.

"What's a bed jacket?" I asked, scanning the clothes list.

"A cardigan worn in bed," Mum explained. I'll knit one for you in blue."

She ordered a batch of Cash's name tapes with my name woven in yellow into each strip of fabric and when they arrived, she sewed one on each piece of my clothing.

"Do you have to sew one on my shoe cleaning kit?"

"No, darling. If you like you can write your name in ink on the brushes!"

I liked having my name on everything, sewn in.

IT TOOK me completely unawares. I was alright travelling with Mum on the Paddy to London but when it was time to leave her at Paddington Station and go off on my own, it hit me. It wasn't helped by the wailing of another girl near us. "Oh, my goodness!" said Mum. "What a din!" Intense emotion rather embarrassed her. "Couldn't she be less noisy?" Evidently, Deborah — I found out her name later — couldn't.

Tears welled in my eyes and my chest heaved but I never asked Mum to take me home or return me to Penninghame School.

The train shunted into the station and its doors opened. Mum helped me in to search for a compartment with other girls going to Badminton School. They were easy to spot. We wore the same uniform: an air force blue tweed overcoat with a brown felt hat. Beneath my coat I wore a white vest, a white blouse, a light blue tunic, beige socks, and brown leather pumps.

"Goodbye, darling!" Mum whispered, after planting a kiss on my cheek. Making her way out of the compartment, she left the train and gave me a brief wave before she disappeared down the platform. I couldn't stop crying then. What might happen now and how would I cope? I wasn't very old and didn't know anyone at my new school yet, except the stuffy, old head-mistress.

With one of my twenty-four hankies, I wiped my eyes and nose. "Come here!" said an older girl. "It's not as bad as that!"

She pulled me onto her knee and wiped my right cheek with her hanky.

"I don't want to cry but..." I burst into tears again.

"You'll be okay. The Junior School's fine. They're nice there with Spikey; she's the head matron."

In the compartment were three other girls, cracking jokes with each other. I listened. "You went abroad?" said one with hundreds of freckles. "You lucky thing! Where?"

"Majorca!" replied a slim girl with fair hair.

"Wow! It's alright for some! We only went to Pontypool!"

"I got to London!" added a tubby girl with frizzy, brown hair.

"We saw the Changing of the Guard at Buckingham Palace and then we went to the theatre!"

"What did you see?"

"The King and I."

"What's that about?"

"A governess falling for an emperor in Siam, wherever that is."

"Sounds like a Chinese Jane Eyre. Is it?"

When I arrived at the Junior School I found Spikey, holding a large list. "So, who are you?" she asked.

"Mary!" I replied in a whisper.

"Mary what?" demanded Spikey. "You are not the only Mary here, you know!"

"Gladstone," I said quietly. Although Spikey was small, no taller than me, she wasn't friendly.

"You're in here," she said. "Dormitory 5. The small one with Sarah and Frances. They know the ropes, so they'll see you right!"

I pushed my way into the room, then took the vacant bed opposite the door. Sarah offered to show me around rhe room. There was a piano in the corner and a locker by our beds for personal belongings.

"Let's go outside!" suggested my companion. At the back of the school building was a large, metal climbing frame and, tucked in a corner by a laurel, a small, circular pond, its water covered with weeds. Staring down, I noticed someone standing beside me, mirrored in the water. A girl dressed in the same uniform as I wore but her face, arms and legs were dark brown.

"What's your name? She asked with a smile.

"Mary!"

"Mine's Fatima. If I stand on that," she pointed to the pond, "will I sink?"

I nodded and said, "You'd better not!"

Fatima had flown from Nigeria to be a pupil at Badminton School. When her father visited, he wore a long white robe and a small hat embroidered in many colours.

That evening, we formed a queue in the corridor to enter the dining room but not before we each pulled on an overall; some girls wore them in emerald green and others in sapphire blue. "It's to protect your uniform. You don't want to spill gravy over your nice new tunic, do you?" Spikey advised.

The following morning, I met Miss Pitt, the Junior School head-teacher. "Welcome, Mary!" she smiled. "You've come a long way, haven't you?" Two days later, I received my first letter from home. It was from Dad but I couldn't read his writing. Ever since his accident with the combine harvester, his hand-writing was nearly illegible.

So, Spikey read the letter out to me. "My dear Mary", it began. "I'm glad you arrived safely. I'm sure you'll enjoy yourself soon and make friends. Try hard to be brave. The vet told us yesterday that although Cara made a bed for her puppies under the spinet, she's not expecting. It's what they call 'a phantom pregnancy'. I'm coming to take you out on October 12th and Mummy will be down for half term. Much love, Daddy"

It wasn't long before Sarah and Frances in the dorm ganged up on me. "Crying's wet!" declared Frances. As her parents lived in Venezuela where her father worked for Shell, she'd been in the school since nursery and was used to being away from home.

"So, stop it!" she snapped.

"She's right! It's feeble to cry. You're like Maureen in Form B," added Sarah. "You don't want to be like her, blubbing all the time. Buck up, Mary!"

The twelve week term stretched out endlessly before me. Each night in the dorm I suffered Sarah and Frances's bullying.

"That's what happens when you're a new girl," announced Frances as she pinched me on my arm. "You have to put up with it." So, I let them send me to Coventry. I knew about people being sent to Siberia, where it was miserable and cold, but not to Coventry really. I soon found out it meant being cold-shouldered.

Frances and Sarah talked to each other after lights out and ignored me. I turned my face to the wall and imagined myself in my bedroom at home, with the moon's rays shining through the gaps in the curtains. I saw myself approach my chest-of-drawers, lean over it, part the curtains and gaze at my hill. If I kept my eyes shut and ignored these girls, I could see it, green in spring, purple in late summer and brown with white speckles in winter. Too often, though, they'd interrupt my dreams.

"Where did you say you came from?" asked Sarah.

"Scotland."

"Oh!" she giggled. "That's where men wear skirts!"

"Say, 'Och, aye, the noo, Mary! Come on," they jeered.

"You don't sound Scottish!"

I'd heard that remark before and had learned to parry it with "I was born in England. My parents speak without an accent."

Frances and Sarah got me to run errands for them. "Go and get the mop," they demanded. "And give me one of your sweeties!" ordered Sarah after we lined up on the stairs for our daily quota, of four boiled sweets, two chocolates, and two pear drops. Frances came up, demanding I hand them over. I refused and stuffed all four sweets into my mouth at once.

"You'll pay for that," she said threateningly.

I've no idea how I managed that first term, but it was wonderful when it ended. Mum's cousin, Bride Binney picked me up in her Mini and drove me all the way home. This was especially kind, since, at eighteen months, after watching her pick daisies and delphiniums in our garden before we moved to Scotland, I spat at her. It was my way of saying how angry I was that she, an adult and a lady, whose husband, an admiral, had been Governor of Tasmania, was allowed to pick flowers when I was not.

My favourite pastime then was picking snowdrops under the hedge, daffodils on the lawn, ladies' smock in rough grass, buttercups in the fields and bluebells in the woods. I didn't see a difference between the flowers you were allowed to pick and those you weren't.

We arrived home in the dark and I rushed to Lis and Janet's bedroom. I wanted to kiss them but was embarrassed by my tears. I couldn't stop them streaming down my cheeks. I was proud of having survived boarding school, in having been launched into a strange world or, to be more exact, pitched into it.

Returning home was difficult though. The animals were wary

of me, treating me like a visitor. Cara, who reserved her snapping for strangers, growled at me. The ponies, Marty in particular, refused to be caught even though I offered her a sugar lump. Mrs Sykes didn't know what to say as she vacuumed the dining room. I'd already lost touch with Melanie and realised that the only friends I could make here were children of my parents' friends.

By the end of the first week of the holidays, I felt I no longer belonged in Wigtownshire. Lis and Janet played together and were very close and Colin, who was four years old, was their mascot; not mine.

Attending Badminton School had made heavy demands on me. I should've stayed at home and travelled to Penninghame School. Instead, my parents got me to make a premature journey toward adulthood. I wasn't old enough to cope really.

Lounging on his favourite armchair with his stool before him, Dad said, "Everyone we know does it".

"The Spartans did it," Mum added, inspecting her tea spoons, and muttering that they should not have been used to eat boiled eggs as the silver became tarnished.

"Who were they?" I asked.

"Citizens of a city-state in Ancient Greece! Even their girls were tough, wrestling bears and the like!"

"Would I have made a good Spartan?" I asked.

Mum shook her head. "You're too emotional! A stiff upper lip is the name of the game for them and people like us. In Israel too, children are put into institutions all day, away from their parents."

"Why?"

"To toughen them up."

Why must we become tough, I wondered? What's the point?

Christmas arrived and went. On the 27th we attended the Pony Club Dance in Newton Stewart's Crown Hotel where Mr Drem arrived 'very fu'. He was completely sozzled. He made a bee-line for any young girl who didn't manage to run away quickly enough. I was in his line of fire now. Bleary eyed, he lurched to me and grasped my right hand. His other arm hooked tightly my waist. "Come oan, lass. Tak' a turn aroon the room wi yer Uncle Alec.

There's a girl!" I stumbled around a couple of chairs, while turning my head as far from his as I could, particularly his mouth that stank of whisky. It made me feel sick. "There ye are. You're no a bad wee dancer, Miss. And I'm no bad neither. Alec Drem's got mair talent than jist selling tapioca and blood oranges. He can do a fair rumba. I'm no bad at the tango either. Want a try?" he said and pushed me, back first, towards the dance floor. "No!" I cried. I tore away from him and ran from the room.

Apart from Alec Drem, the Christmas holiday went well, but I dreaded the day when I had to return to Badminton School. This time I travelled to Bristol with Petronella, a girl from the Lake District, who wore her hair in a long, single pigtail. As the train drew into Oxenholme platform, I saw her with her parents. Her father's posture was ram-rod straight. He was a retired colonel.

My second term wasn't easier than the first but Miss Pitt, in seeing how sad I looked before, tried to find ways of making me happier. The fact I was Scottish was not lost on her. She drew me aside to tell me she had planned a school assembly on Robert Burns. 25th January was the bicentenary of his birth, and she wanted me to recite one of his poems. Ignoring 'Tam O'Shanter' and Dad's favorite, 'Epistle to Davy', I settled for 'My Luve's like a Red, Red Rose' because it was easy to learn.

In our dormitory a new girl, Anna, took Sarah's place. Sadly, I'm ashamed to admit, I, the abused, turned proud abuser. I gave Anna the same kind of treatment I had received from Frances and Sarah. Poor Anna! Her father was a bishop. She took it all silently, just turning the other cheek. To visit her, her father dressed in a frock coat and black breeches.

By the time the summer term arrived, my homesickness and misery warped into anger. I wasn't exactly a delinquent, as they termed intractable children, but I was disobedient and feckless. At least my antics challenged those seemingly caring for us.

Princess Margaret's wedding to Anthony Armstrong Jones was a public holiday, and all of us in the Junior School spent the day at Longleat. No hippos stalked its lakes and no lions yet prowled its parkland, but the stately home there had opened to us.

Towards the end of the summer term I ended up in bad odour after Frances, Anna and I organised a midnight feast. Going to bed and having 'lights out' at 7.45 pm, it was hard to stay awake until midnight. At 10.45 pm, we switched on the light and spread our spoils on the bedspread: six boiled sweets reserved from our rations; a stale crust of bread; a couple of apples, and a few broken biscuits. Within five minutes, Spikey discovered us.

"You'll never hear the end of this!" she said. We didn't. For the following seven nights, we had to go to bed at 6.00 pm.

My next term in the Junior School I bedded down in a large dormitory with five others. Catching the train from Carlisle, I arrived at the school late in the evening, and was surprised to find that Julia, a new girl, was as tall as I was. We became firm friends. Although she lived in London with her mother, brother and sisters, we had something more in common: she hadn't been privately educated before arriving at Badminton.

She was the perfect catalyst for my rebelliousness.

Miss Pitt could see it coming and tried to divert us by interesting us in the poet laureate, John Masefield, and soon enough I could recite "I must go down to the sea again..." by heart.

Had I known how uncomplimentary Masefield was about my grandfather, I might not have been so keen. In 1915, during the Great War, when the two men worked as orderlies in a hospital in north-east France, Masefield described my mother's father as 'a public school type, tall and stone deaf, who follows me around like a faithful dog'.

Miss Pitt suggested that, in early June for Masefield's birthday, we write him a poem. Poor man!. We composed one as a joint effort and got back an individually signed card of thanks from him, together with a copy of one of his lectures on Keats and Shelley.

To keep us further occupied, Miss Pitt introduced us to the Derbyshire practise of well-dressing, where pictures are made of biblical scenes with flowers placed on a bed of moist clay.

But even the poet laureate and the well-dressing couldn't distract Julia and me from our subversive activities: talking for hours after lights out, wandering out of the narrow bounds of the school wall or hedge, and committing other misdemeanours.

Keeping close tabs on us wasn't all due to prissiness. Badminton School, it seemed, was a paedophile's mecca, I now knew that term. Senior School pupils slept in the main school building, but also in a number of houses outside it. To reach their dormitories, girls trudged down paths and lanes in the dark. One house was in nearby St Monica's, a large Church of England home for elderly women. Local flashers had wind of our school and positioned themselves behind the hedge below the Junior School and did their best to frighten us. No teacher, however, briefed, consoled or enlightened us on what was happening. We were left in the dark on our own.

Etching by Lis Gladstone in the manner of
David S Gladstone's award-winning work
at Eton

— Shocks —

TOWARDS THE END OF THE TERM, my parents warned me of events by letter. They weren't allowed to phone except in emergencies and for some reason, Mum didn't think my pet's injury was urgent. She said, she didn't want to alarm me while I was away at school, but when I arrived home for the summer holidays, I saw that Jura, my Jack Russell terrier, had lost her right eye. I rushed upstairs and burst into tears. I didn't want to let Mum see how upset I was as she felt guilty enough. Jura wasn't right. Something had gone that would never come back. She was no longer the beautiful dog I knew. It had happened on sports day at Hartfield: Mum was to drive to Ayr to watch Janet, excellent at running, win all the races there. Mum didn't make it. Cara and Breck, the two big dogs, had a fearsome fight in the kitchen, and Mum grabbed a broom and hit them hard. Jura dashed into the fray, but Mum failed to see in time and clipped her on the eye.

There were other animal disasters: when Patsy's foal broke its leg, Mum sent it away, never revealing what happened. Out of sight out of mind was how our parents dealt with tragedy. Everything in our lives was meant to be ironed out.

The next shock was my school report. It wasn't just bad. It was appalling. Worst of all was how Miss Pitt believed I was 'easily led'. That hurt. I wouldn't have minded so much if she had accused me of malevolence or cunning but she saw me as weak and malleable. "Mary will never be a leader. She is too easily influenced by others," she wrote.

I wasn't sure whether I wanted to lead people, but I certainly didn't wish to be led. I liked having a close friend, like Julia, but if truth be known, I preferred being on my own, reading a book or listening to a record disc on the player, but at school they did not allow us to be on our own. We were supervised in the playground and required to sleep in a dormitory.

Mum ordered me to my room to discuss my bad report.

"What's wrong, Mary?" she asked in a voice, half accusing and half concerned. "Aren't you happy there?"

The idea of telling her what I really thought about the school was not an option. To attend Douglas Ewart in Newton Stewart and admit I couldn't stomach boarding school, would be to admit failure. "I'll grow into it!" I volunteered, hoping my Badminton experience was like a pair of shoes too large or a book I wasn't mature enough to understand yet.

"Well," said Mum, tossing the report into the waste paper basket, "Let's turn over a new leaf and say nothing more about it! Would you like macaroni cheese or egg and cheese flan for lunch?"

I didn't want either but I chose macaroni.

The third shock wasn't exactly a surprise. I anticipated it. The lady who led the pony club camp held me in total disdain, though I didn't know why. Maybe my new horse, Loppy, annoyed her. Being 15 hands high, Loppy was strictly speaking not a pony but a horse. Loppy was, in many respects, a bit loopy. As big as a mule's, her long ears wouldn't stand up properly. They fell over her eyes onto her forehead. Her name, Loppy Lugs, referred to her ears. She was badly co-ordinated. At pony club meetings, she never fell in line during our drills when we walked, trotted and cantered around the arena marked out on the grass with oil drums. She couldn't easily jump obstacles. In the end, Mum surmised that there was something wrong with her sight, her loppy lugs getting in the way. Mum had bought Loppy because she was cheap as Dad did not like spending money on horses and their paraphernalia.

My appearance at the camp on Loppy always infuriated the pony club lady. This time, when all the girls, who boarded in a cheese loft on the farm where the camp was held, were tucked up in camp beds and about to go to sleep, I had a disagreement with one of the camp lady's daughters. At lunch-time, the following day, without allowing me to state my side of the argument, she and her husband publicly humiliated me, first alluding to my bad school report, then my behaviour and my hopeless equestrian skills. I saw no benefit in trying to enlist Mum's support. I knew she wouldn't defend me.

Our progression to the Senior School spelled a new-found freedom though. One of our privileges was to keep pets: white mice, a hamster, a rabbit or guinea pig. Julia and I decided on a couple of guinea pigs which Mum bought from a shop in Wigtown. We gave them the pretentious names of Eine (the female) and Kleine (the male). Their surname, yes, was Nachtmusik, after Mozart's chamber piece, 'a little serenade'. But the Nachtmusiks soon bred. Their litter was huge and hungry and they used up all our pocket money in fodder. I found a solution albeit a dishonest one. Remembering Peter Rabbit in Mr McGregor's garden, I ran to a small cabbage patch close to the bursar's house, looked to see if anyone was near, and ripped up a cabbage from the earth. I hid it under my coat and, when inside the pet shed where all the livestock was housed, I slipped my booty into the Nachtmusik's hutch. The hungry family devoured the cabbage before I managed to close the pet shed door. Repeated, this was a reasonable scheme considering the demands of nine mouths, but there was a drawback. The Nachtmusiks wouldn't eat the cabbage stalks. Occasionally a draconian matron called Phoebe, inspected the pet shed. If anyone were to discover felonies such as the one I had committed, it would be her. From across any room, no matter how large, Phoebe could detect a whiff of forbidden scent or a hint of mascara or lipstick. Luckily, fortune was with me. I was safe.

In Group 2 of the Senior School (Group 1 was the top form of the Junior) there was a large intake of nice, new blood: Lesley Bennun, a South African girl whose family escaped Verwoerd's apartheid system, and Catherine Joachim, whose father taught in a Cumberland Quaker school, especially. When, on the first day of the term Catherine revealed that she came from Wigton, I wondered if we were unknown neighbours, as I lived five miles from Wigtown, but was disappointed to discover that an expanse of estuary, the Solway, separated us. Of the other new girls, plenty came from London and the South East. But some were from more exotic places: a Chinese girl from New York and two sisters from Brazil. One girl sang like a lark.

There were even aristocratic twins whose aunt taught Latin, chain-smoked, and kept a large poodle. Then Polly Toynbee. The first thing I noticed was her name. I liked it not only for the song.

"Polly, put the kettle on!" but because the original Polly was a name for the humble, for women who served. Hence the song. Even at eleven years old, Polly Toynbee seemed to be destined for important things. I didn't know at first about her grandfather, Arnold, the historian, nor her father, Philip, the journalist, but once in the Junior School, when we were drying our hair in Spikey's room before the gas fire, Polly proudly told me her parents were divorced. This was pronounced in a way to encourage me to feel that children from her kind of family enjoyed a freedom from secrecy and hypocrisy that offspring from my kind did not.

During our first term in Group 2 on a Monday evening after supper at 7 pm, we went to Miss Sanderson or BMS's study, the only carpeted room in the school, and listened to her reading 'Pride and Prejudice', so I came to associate Jane Austen with my headmistress. The early novel developed as a study in etiquette for young women. Perhaps the idea behind BMS's weekly readings of the book was to prepare us for marriage to a well-heeled man. While we listened, we either sewed or knitted.

Although we had a well-stocked library at Badminton, I lost my appetite for reading. Miss Pitt tried to encourage me to read John Buchan, "The Thirty-Nine Steps" in particular, because part of it is set in Galloway but I couldn't get through it.

Mummy steered me away from Enid Blyton and presented me instead with an assortment of authors who wrote about animals. Kipling was one. I'd been brought up on Mowgli but she gave me 'Stalky & Co'. I had little desire to identify with an Edwardian public schoolboy, when the sun had almost entirely set on the Empire. Even to me, Kipling cut a forlorn and dated figure. More dated and suspect was Henry Williamson. I hadn't the heart to read his 'Tarka the Otter' because I knew it would be sad. In the same vein was Anna Sewell's 'Black Beauty' which charts the career, from easy youth to the down-trodden end of a carriage-horse. An even sadder tale was 'The Story of a Young Deer'. Why Mum wished me to read stories about animal abuse is anyone's guess.

In the Senior School our dormitories were larger and more plentiful, but during the summer term I became ill and was so poorly that the school sent me to the first floor of the main building where the San (sanatorium) was. It consisted of a collection of small rooms with a bed in each. During my last term in the Junior school, I had also suffered from flu and stayed in the San. As I was recovering, I had a good view one Friday evening of the hall opposite. Group 6, the school leavers, were having a party and dancing with senior boys from Clifton College. This time, in the San, I listened to radio bulletins of the American Presidential campaign. The protagonists were Richard Nixon and J.F. Kennedy, but I found it hard to distinguish whose voice belonged to whom and had no idea what Democrats or Republicans meant. I was not interested in adult politics. Hearing about the Cold War, I saw that the West viewed Russia as the bogey, but America was too remote for me to take seriously.

Our doctor was Dr Tryon. We called her Tripod. She wore a grey suit or, as Mum described it, a coat and skirt, had mannish, cropped hair, and carried a brown Gladstone bag that matched her brogues. Although her manner was abrupt, her voice was more gentle, and her quiet tone inspired confidence. She was the first woman I met who seemed to possess kindness and brains.

I was lucky not to fall ill very often at Badminton, as life there wasn't easy. None of the staff ever singled me out for attention or praise. Instead, I struggled with my studies, particularly with Latin, although they put me in the top group for this subject. I was not successful with my parsing, declensions or conjugations. Miss Jeffrey, who was called Jappy because on her first day at Badminton she wore a cotton dress printed with japonicas, was oblivious of me and others in the class. She stood before us, her eyes closed, spouting stories on ancient Rome, about Romulus and Remus, the twins who sucked the teats of a kindly she-wolf. The idea revolted me. It had never occurred to me in my wildest dreams to suck the teats of Cara, Jura or Breck, my female dogs who were not unlike a wolf. Jappy tried to get us to distinguish between the Greek names for the Gods and the Roman. She also told us how the Romans regarded politics and their system of Government. When Arabella and Sybella, both the brainiest girls in our supposedly brainy Latin group, raised the question of freedom for women, Jappy opened one eye, usually her left, rather like an owl, and shut it quickly. "Very little!"

She taught us many marvellous Roman poets: her favorite, Horace, the king of poets Virgil, Catullus, and others. Jappy tasked us with reading passages from Ovid's 'Metamorphosis, while explaining the background to Philemon and Baucis, the old couple who welcomed the gods when they went begging and Atalanta, an ace runner who outshone all men on the track until Hippomenes tricked her to run off it, but for me, Ovid was a dead poet who wore, I assumed, a long, white dress or toga similar to the outfits we created out of bed sheets and well-placed pins.

This garb was created for our 'orgies' arranged by Jappy. She loved to talk of orgies, but never alluded to sex. The Badminton staff, especially BMS, didn't believe in sex, it seemed, except for 'the other classes' or within the bounds of marriage. Orgies to Jappy meant an excess of food and wine and a way to liven up a dead language. Fiendishly difficult, it was like working a crossword, where all words were placed in order: adverbs here, prepositions there and the verb, like a lost universal aunt, tucked at the end of a sentence.

If Jappy sailed close to the wind with her allusions to the Roman orgy, my English teacher, Miss Franklin, a diminutive lady, dealt with sexual misdemeanour in a more perfunctory manner. For one of our preps, we had to search our anthology, choose a poem, learn it by heart, and recite it during the next class. I found Shakespeare's Sonnets, 5 and 18. No! Everyone learned them. I wasn't all that interested in poetry, but I liked Rupert Brooke for his handsome face. Then I found a poem by John Betjeman. Mum and Dad had a new volume of his poetry. His rhyming verse with a jaunty rhythm was about girls on ponies at gymkhanas and jejune romance. Dad laughed at 'Come friendly bombs and fall on Slough, It isn't fit for humans now.' He also appreciated Betjeman's love of architecture but his poem that most attracted me concerned Oscar Wilde and his arrest at the Cadogan Hotel. It was easy to learn and it even had a bit of dialogue to pepper it up. Although a Scot, I found Cockney an easy accent to mimic and had the poem learned within half an hour. In class I rose to my feet, announcing its title. Miss Franklin stared at me angrily. "How did that poem come to be in a school anthology?" she asked rhetorically. She allowed me to recite the poem and the class were wild with appreciation. They even asked for an encore, which I obligingly gave. Then came a question from clever Arabella and the even cleverer Sybella.

"Why did they arrest him?" I had wanted to know too. When the policeman in the poem proclaimed that he was 'taking Wilde to a place where felons and criminals dwell', I wondered why Wilde, the famous playwright, had to go.

"Now," said Miss Franklin, slamming shut her book, "Close your anthologies. Open your grammar. Today we'll work on adverbs."

If Miss Franklin was frightening, then Mme Thorak, our French teacher, was terrifying. From the front of the classroom, she fixed dawdlers and slouches with her gimlet stare. MT soon got us all speaking and miming French. We learned expressive hand gestures, a Gallic shrug, and to talk in a perfect Parisian accent. The snag was I understood little of what I was saying.

MT saw to it that nobody, after Lesson 2, dared pronounce a 'u' as 'ou'. As for that 'r', the bane of Anglophones, I couldn't manage it. My 'r' sounded like the gasp of an expiring fish. How could a strip of water, expropriated by us as the English Channel, result in such different languages: one with diphthongs uttered in the back of the mouth, while the other with none was spat out from the front.

MT polluted one of our few pleasures, by making us speak French at table on Wednesdays. We all prayed not to sit next to her, but MT, of course, could hear a mis-pronunciation from the end of any long table.

"Le pain!" she would shout. "Qui a dit la pain? Non, non, non, remarquez, c'est LE pain!"

To my surprise, Scotland was never mentioned in history class, At Penninghame, it was. I'd learned all about my past. At Bad: minton, we memorised only the English kings from William the Conqueror to Henry VIII, by chanting rhythmically, to eke out any potential rhyme: Willie, Willie, Harry, Steve, Harry, Dick, John, Harry 3. Teddy, Teddy, Teddy, Dick, Harry 4, 5 and 6.

Except that Teddy 1 was not a harmless, cuddly figure but a brute, known north of the Border as 'The Hammer of the Scots'. That I already knew.

I learned the king's dates separately: 1066-1087, 1087-1100 1100-1135, 1135-1154. The early Normans enjoyed long reigns, but it was a risky ploy remembering like this. If I muddled up or missed out a set, my edifice fell. It didn't help either, when in English, Miss Franklin introduced us to Henry V. Shakespeare complicated matters. Laying aside the Pucks, Oberons, Malvolios, Portias and Shylocks, he meddled with history.

"A mere propagandist!" Miranda announced. We all knew she was the mouthpiece for her father, an Oxford don. In my heart, I agreed. If "Macbeth" was anything to go by, Shakespeare would never have found a job with the Scottish Tourist Board. We were not all power-hungry murderers, wanting the crown.

As for my lacking performance in Maths and the sciences, it seemed, Mrs Dunlop's influence damaged me irrevocably. I found geometry and algebra incomprehensible. In biology, our teacher only gave us a coy excursion into human reproduction sandwiched between plant osmosis and the breathing system of the tadpole. The nearest we got to sexual reality was to draw the testes, ure-thra and penis for the male, and the Fallopian tubes, ovaries, cervix and vagina for the female. Our biology teacher, Miss Stan-ley, failed to explain how the male body parts fitted into the parts of the female for what she termed 'love-making'. Referring to the activity as 'having sex' was unthinkable. Instead, we alluded to 'doing that' or 'making babies'.

Our class was little the wiser about variations, aberrations and oddities, so we went to the library on our own. The encyclopedia should have helped, but wasn't graphic enough.

Dad bought a Penguin paperback of D.H. Lawrence's 'Lady Chatterley's Lover', with an image of a phoenix on the front cover, because Lawrence modelled Sir Clifford Chatterley, the crippled aristocrat, on one of the Sitwells, who we were related to by marriage. I scoured its pages but couldn't work out what Lawrence was getting at and what Mellors had done with Constance Chatterley that was so frightful.

Julia, though, returned from the summer holidays with 'The Kama Sutra', which Miss Derry, our house-mistress, promptly confiscated. Julia's divorced mother campaigned for nuclear disarmament and was part of the Anti Apartheid movement, but she did not have a second copy of the book. Nor did the library carry it.

The following year, while studying for our GCE Ordinary levels, we saw newspaper photographs of two pretty girls: Christine Keeler and Mandy Rice-Davies. Referred to as 'call girls', they were mixed up in a court case involving a Russian spy and John Profumo, a government minister, but I didn't quite understand what these women had done wrong.

"They were prostitutes," explained Miranda. "Men pay them to do it, you know what I mean!"

Miranda saw herself as an authority on sex and claimed she knew all about homosexuality too.

"The ancient Greeks had boyfriends."

"If that was true, how did they not all die out?"

"They had both. Boyfriends and wives."

"Just like my Uncle Bert!" piped up Margaret.

That made me wonder. Without boys and without learning to be with them, how could we be expected to live with them, and 'do that', perfectly, forever.

— Going Out —

WHAT MADE BADMINTON SCHOOL tolerable was getting out of it, legitimately or otherwise. I had few relations living in the south of England, so Granny took it upon herself to find someone in the family, no matter how distant, to take me out. She came up with Winifred Hayter, her niece and her brother, Ivan's daughter, who lived in Portishead near Bristol and had no car. Unlike my other relatives, the Hayters weren't rich. Neither had they a television. When I first visited by bus, we sat in the living room and listened to a radio show, The Goons. I liked their daughter, Gillian, who went to a rival Bristol school. Mr Hayter, however, wore a sneer whenever he spoke to me, asking me questions about my father's possessions. How many acres did he farm? How many cows did he own? How many cars? What make were they and how old?

My most embarrassing moment was yet to come. After a visit to Portishead, I travelled back to school by bus, accompanied by Winifred. I needed a bathroom but didn't dare tell my cousin. I managed until we reached the outskirts of Bristol but could not hold on any longer, and wet my pants and the seat. The next time I visited, Winifred sent me to the loo before we left the house.

While I was still in the Junior School, the Whitehorns took me out. Alan Whitehorn met Mum on a Greek cruise early in 1939 just before she was to go up to Somerville College, Oxford. Her brother, Jock and sister-in-law, Anne, were on a skiing holiday in Austria, gallivanting about right up until War was declared.

Alan Whitehorn taught in a public school. He'd kept in touch with Mum. He and his wife rented a flat in Bristol's Clifton area. One Sunday they took me out for lunch. Mrs Whitehorn was deaf, which sent me into a fluster. Never having had to deal directly with this kind of impairment, I tried to speak clearly so that Mrs W could lip-read my words. She couldn't, but she showed me a photograph on their mantelpiece of a young woman in her wedding dress: Katherine, who wrote for The Observer. After lunch, Alan took me to the zoo. He was good at entertaining children.

"What books do you read?" he asked as we left the reptile house. One was 'Redcap Runs Away', a book set in the Middle Ages. He was reading 'Ring of Bright Water' about a man who kept otters at a croft in the Scottish Highlands. I'd tried to read it but had skipped the long adjectives, the pages on natural history, and had only looked briefly at the black and white photographs.

During my first year in the Senior School, Mum's older sister, Douna, and her husband, Henry, came to live in Bristol. I hardly knew these relatives as we saw little of them as they previously had been sheep farmers near Lochgilphead in Argyll. Henry was an Ang-lican clergyman but had lost his faith after his war experiences when, as an army chaplain, he was captured and imprisoned in Italy. In his fifties, he re-affirmed his faith and worked as an industrial chaplain in the Clyde shipyards. With his Old Etonian accent and genteel ways, he might have cut a ridiculous figure, but satisfied his colleagues in physical strength and gained their respect. As a sheep farmer he had tramped daily uphill and down, and was, for his age, extremely fit.

Originally a curate in East London's Peckham, Henry had found nothing suitable in the Scottish Episcopal church, when he decided to return to parish work. So the couple travelled south to a parish at St Mary Redcliffe in Bristol. Douna wouldn't think of moving without bringing one of her dogs. A photo showed her, wearing a cloche hat, in charge of a dozen spaniels. Douna kept dogs in packs. Like other Argyll farmers, she worked with collies training them to round up sheep. Douna seemed a wild bird, a stonechat or lapwing, trapped in her husband's cage.

The first time I went out with Douna and Henry, I felt painfully shy and spoke very little. They drove me to Chewton Mendip, and Wells and Yeovil where we stopped for afternoon tea in a hotel. My aunt and uncle asked me out often, but I wasn't entirely relaxed with them, Still I liked my family living nearby. BMS had her eye on Henry for another purpose. She wanted him to conduct a school service. Our establishment was non-denominational and girls of all religions, or none, were welcome, but it preferred the preaching of an Anglican clergyman, the odd Franciscan or even a nun or two. Henry was therefore an ideal target. He realised what he was letting himself in for when he agreed to take our Sunday evening service. From the start, it was embarrassing as he spoke in such a soft voice that few people could hear him. Some yawned, others coughed and fidgeted. A few at the back of the hall, played noughts and crosses with pencils on the back cover of their hymn books.

"What an intimidating congregation!" Henry said afterwards when I met him outside. I didn't have the courage to ask what 'intimidating' meant to him but during our cocoa break, the hot drink supplied before bed-time, I consulted my dictionary.

My uncle's next visit was much more challenging to me. Polly Toynbee organised a 'Ban the Bomb' debate in our school hall and invited pupils from other Bristol schools to attend. In 1962 we were in the throes of the first wave of the campaign. Two years earlier, I visited Trafalgar Square, with Julia and her mother, where we demonstrated against the bomb but our protest wasn't committed enough for us to 'sit down'. Nor did we come across Canon Collins or Bertrand Russell: both were present. For her debate, Polly and Julia arranged a spokesman for the anti-nuclear lobby while BMS roped in Henry for the pro-bomb camp. They didn't care if a pro-bomber spoke but BMS did. The school's reputation, as a fine example of liberal education, might blow up in her face.

I considered boycotting the debate. That my uncle would lose was a foregone conclusion. He was set up for, if not Armageddon, then at least his Waterloo, and was unaware of this, it seemed.

I sat in the hall on a canvas seat, waiting for him to enter the stage. The CND speaker began the discussion, his facts laced with spine-chilling details of what a nuclear winter might be like. Then Henry rose to offer his views, with no facts at his fingertips, but only memories of his war, to explain why he did not want to ban the bomb. "Believe me, war is terrible. I've been through one and seen things I can't even begin to describe. We need the atom bomb to maintain our hard-won peace," he concluded.

Then the debate opened up for the audience contribution. Up stood a girl from Clifton High School, who asked why Henry a-greed with the Bomb. "I don't understand how you, as a minister of religion, want it." She spoke softly, expressing her thoughts gently but firmly, in a manner that was incredulous, not querulous.

Up until then, I had followed my parents' and relatives' views unquestioningly. With people opposing Henry, I felt I was being attacked. Yet, the girl's reasoning and manner impressed me. Henry was neither uneducated or stupid, but he was a believer in fighting for a better world, as he saw it, and required no more reason than that.

This event was a watershed. Our family patriarch had met his match. I was mortified that a softly-spoken, articulate girl had challenged my uncle, and he did not have a good answer.

Another questioner stood up and lambasted Harold McMillan but Henry promptly defended the Prime Minister. "He's a decent chap, I was at Eton with him!" This was my cue to hang my head in shame. I had enough sense to understand that my uncle had gone too far this time. Nobody, in their right senses should utter Eton, that four letter word to a roomful of left wing protesters.

Within a couple of years, my uncle and aunt left Bristol and settled in a parish outside Swindon where they accommodated ex-prisoners in the vicarage itself, until the residents of the sleepy village objected. So, they moved to the center of Swindon. I never entirely recovered from witnessing Henry's humiliation during the 'ban the bomb' conference. .

Badminton School organized educational outings too. Coach loads of girls, supervised by a staff member, attended performances at the Bristol Old Vic repertory company. I sat through several bad Shakespearean productions of the history plays.

"One soldier winked at me from the stage!" said Sybella.

"A Hotspur lieutenant smiled at me in Act 2!" said Arabella, who couldn't let her friend upstage her.

The Bristol Old Vic repertoire was mainly Shaw, Chekhov and Shakespeare. For a while I was keen on music and fantasised about playing the violin in an orchestra, even the unimpressive Bristol-based 'The Paragon', that played at Colston Hall. I liked classical music, particularly Mozart, Berlioz, and Wagner. I borrowed records from the school library and hid in a music room in the science block to listen to 'Tannhauser' and 'The flying Dutchman'. For a knowing, lonely, pubescent girl like me, Wagner was a tonic in spite of his dubious political affiliations.

It was too far to travel home for half term. Before Douna and Henry arrived in Bristol, I stayed with Jean, Dad's older sister, and her husband, Roddie in Buckinghamshire. Recently returned from Copenhagen where he was British ambassador, Roddie was now helping Edward Heath with his negotiations for Britain to enter the Common Market. Uncle Roddie wasn't easy to talk to. His lack of ease with children, according to Dad, could be caused by his childhood, as Gillian, his mother died giving birth to him.

Married to Joseph Gurney Barclay, Gillian and Joseph were evangelical Anglican-Quaker missionaries in Japan. Roddie told me about a train journey he made as a four year old. To while away the time, as they crossed Russia, he played in the corridor with a little Russian girl. This was the only story he ever told me.

Just as I sensed Granny's reservations towards me, I knew Jean loved us, but as extensions of Dad, her younger brother and that she expected us to measure up. Girls should marry 'well' and boys should 'manage' the family business, bank or farm. Our aunt, however, when visiting, brought lovely presents from Copenhagen, like a porcelain statue of 'The Little Mermaid'. She gave us soft toys, paintings, and models of horses too.

One day, on visiting Kailzinet where Jean and Dad grew up, she led us to the top of the house to the nursery where her old toys were stacked on shelves and in cupboards. Jean rummaged through the shelves and found two plaster horses, which she gave to me and Lis. Searching the cupboard, she asked, "Where's the cart? These two ought to be pulling one!"

She showed us why. "Do you see the collar?" she pointed to a protrusion on the horse's neck. "It goes over its head and rests in front of the withers." Jean then explained where the rest of the miniature harness should go: the girth, crupper that encircled the top of the tail, and the breeching strap that ran horizontally around the top of the horse's hind legs to prevent the cart from bumping into its hind quarters. Jean was in her element with horses; her love for them wasn't limited by social considerations. She didn't care about horse-racing or competitive equestrian events. She had an affinity with the animals themselves. Her appreciation was chiefly aesthetic: a miner's pit pony, a polo-player's mount, a thoroughbred show horse, a hunter or garron, working horses like Clydesdales, Suffolk punch or drays that pulled a milkman's float or brewer's lorry — anything equine enthralled her. She fed, groomed, rode, and drove horses in a variety of carts, traps and carriages.

Jean also drew them. When she was a child, the family worshipped on Sundays at Dumfries-shire's Keir kirk. Her artistic attempts are still in the margins of the hymn books' pages. With hymn number 11, in which 'strength' and 'power' are mentioned and not horses, Jean drew a Shetland pony, nuzzling the flank of a Connemara. Hymn number 56 finds a Welsh cob jumping a hedge with a hatless rider. "Though no-one bothered to wear hats in those days!" she confessed. In the 'harvest' section, by hymn number 383, were a couple of Clydesdales, ploughing a furrow, heads bowed. A duck and partridge adorn another page. For the hymn 'As pants the hart for cooling streams / When heated in the chase,' Aunt Jean drew a stag with a full head of antlers, tumbling into a stream. In the margin beside it was a crude drawing of a pair of pants and a heart with an arrow through it. Clearly, Jean hadn't added them. It must have been Dad or Jim, his brother.

Jean wasn't religious, so she didn't sketch lambs, donkeys, or fish but painted shepherds warming their hands by a fire for 'While Shepherds watched their flocks by night' in her Christmas carol missal. If the subject were happier, she would have found The Four Horsemen of the Apocalypse ideal. She discovered in the Book of Zechariah that the horses' coats were black, white, dappled or grisled, and bay, and was tempted, as they pulled chariots too, but she learned that the horses signified Conquest, Pestilence, War, Famine and Death and that put her off trying to illustrate them.

It took time for me to get used to Aunt Jean at her home. I was more accustomed to her visiting us at Carsenestock. Along with Roddie and Joe, she brought us southern English sophistication when, in their light, blue Jag, they arrived, slithering through the dung on the road as if they were rolling over a red carpet. Everything at our house fascinated Jean, probably more than her own. Although dairy farming wasn't her prime interest, Jean showed willing, accompanying Dad to the byre, dairy, boiler house, calf-pens, stack-yard, midden, and finishing at the stables.

"Let's see Marty!" Jean suggested. She gave Dad a wink, acknowledging his dislike of horses. "Put them in a field with the cows," he'd complain, "and they'll play havoc!" Dad was correct: ponies sharing a field with cattle bullied them and stole their food.

"You feed, groom and house them," Dad complained, "and all they do is turn round and kick or bite you!"

"Come now, David!" Aunt Jean laughed. "They're prettier than cows."

"Cows mean money in the bank! Horses mean money out of it!" he said.

I liked my aunt and uncle's home, Great White End, an unfortunate name when none of us was all that sylph-like. It was a seventeenth century farm-house, surrounded by a tithe barn, stables, log shed and tack room. Staying there was fun; we ate well, scoffing strawberries grown by Charlie, the gardener, and I liked my cousins. Davina was eight years older than me and, compared to my awkward fourteen year old self, very sophisticated. She was kind and attentive and like a hungry child, I slurped up her warmth. One day she brought me with her upstairs to her room where, on her bed, was a pile of clothes. "These, Mary," she said with a wide smile, "are for you!" As an ambassador's happy daughter, Davina had a wardrobe of lovely skirts, slacks and dresses; my favourite, in pink and white stripes, had a tight-fitting bodice with pencil thin straps and a wide, swirling skirt.

Some of the outfits hardly fitted but I didn't care. They were smart and fashionable and when I wore them I felt like a film star.

Apart from the sexy, striped dress, I loved the velveteen slacks in vibrant abstract colours.

"Here!" Davina showed me a skin-tight pair in black. "Put them on with this!" she said, holding a turquoise blouse with ruffles around the plunging neckline. After I pulled on the clothes, Davina led me to a record player on a low table. From a rack, she selected a disc with a photo of a young bespectacled man on the sleeve. Placing my hands in hers, she ordered me to start dancing as the voice on the disc crooned,

> Well, that'll be the day when you say goodbye,
> Yes, that'll be the day when you make me cry!
> You say you gonna leave, you know it's a lie
> Cause that'll be the day when I die.

I jumped up and down in a stilted manner. Davina undulated her hips gently. "Just feel the beat!" she advised. I could not do it. My movements were hesitant and jerky. My lack of fluidity disappointed me. My cousin tried to console me. "Never mind, Mary! You'll manage it. Just give it time!"

She lifted the arm off the disc, replacing it in its sleeve and banged shut the record player lid. "Come on! Put on your jodhpurs and fetch your hat. We're going for a ride!" Out in the field by the tennis court, we hailed Aunt Jean's hunter and Davina's pony. After catching them, we led horse and pony to the stables where we saddled them up.

Cousins Joe Barclay & Mary Gladstone at Great White End

— THE DUCK BOYS —

WE WERE IN THE FIELD next to the garden and Lis, Janet and I were cracking the ice on the water trough. The first week of the New Year was unusually cold. Janet stopped jumping on the ice, as it wasn't breaking. Sometimes we fell in to the trough and our wellingtons filled up. We caught our breath with the cold, as the icy water seeped into our socks and trousers.

Janet tried to work out which of us had the smallest tummy, or the one that bulged out the least. She pulled down her trousers to just above her knees and there, in the middle of the field, well almost, she asked me to do the same. I declined. I knew mine was larger. I ate more.

Whenever Janet had a chocolate bar, she'd nestle it in her lap or store it away. I'd wolf mine down as soon as I got it. After I finished, my sister brought out her stash to tantalise me with it.

"Guess who's coming tomorrow!" Janet always knew about family events before anyone else. Maybe she had a hotter line than me to the powers-that-be; she certainly commanded the most attention. Lis and I made a number of guesses before we gave up.

"The Duck Boys!" Janet was triumphant. "Dad said!"

"When?"

"Tomorrow!"

Dad coined the name for the four young men from Ayrshire who stayed in his studio or in the old cheese loft above the dairy. They came to shoot wild fowl, like duck and geese. Anyone could walk to the inks and shoot, if they so gruesomely desired, only they had to ask permission from the farmer to cross his fields. As Mum was a bird lover, she persuaded Dad to prevent many wild fowlers from gaining access to the river, but she approved of the Duck Boys, Angus, James, Chris and Patrick. The Solway was renowned for its estuary and migrating birds. The naturalist, Peter Scott,who founded a bird reserve at Slimbridge, had contemplated making our precincts into a bird reserve.

Janet tried to embarrass me. She knew that after Marguerite's, my French exchange's visit in the summer, boys interested me.

How much, I didn't know. The Duck Boys wore cord trousers, tweed jackets, and cloth caps with the brow pulled low over their foreheads, along with stout, brown leather lace-up shoes. Angus was the tallest and I remembered that the previous January, when he returned from a day out with James and Patrick, he looked alright. Better than James with his slowly vanishing acne and overly-big ear lobes and enormous hooked nose.

"You like Chris, don't you?" Janet needled me.

"He's not the handsomest!" said Lis.

"He's the nicest!" I said.

"Can you imagine him doing......"

"What?" asked Lis..

"What all Mum's and Dad's do, you idiot!"

"No," I said. "But I can imagine him kissing me."

"How?"

"With his mouth, of course!"

"On yours?" asked Lis.

"Maybe!" I said.

The Duck boys arrived in an old van. They had cases, bags, guns and all kinds of extras. I saw them when I went to feed the ponies in the field with the muddy track. Dad came out the back door to welcome them, saying he'd seen few greylags or widgeon but he wished the Boys well. I didn't. I couldn't understand how anyone wanted to shoot these birds, but I didn't say so. Mum had the studio ready. She heated it and put out the camp beds. The Boys brought their own bedding.

We saw little of the Duck Boys until they came in for supper. What was obvious was none seem to notice me or my sisters, even when I put on a yellow knitted jumper and curled my hair inwards beneath the chin in the way Marguerite showed me the summer last.

Mum told us that, as it was the holidays, we three could sit with them at dinner. This time it was dinner, and not supper, as we called it usually. Mum gave the Duck Boys a welcoming meal. The main dish was a brace of pheasants from the Buchan-Hepburns, with a few pigeons from Charlie Smith, a reformed poacher. Before we ate, we gathered in the sitting room where I drank tonic water in a large cut glass. The Duck Boys had a glass of sherry. Only Patrick dared ask for a gin and tonic.

Mum and Dad drank whisky, poured through a measure that looked like the shiny, red beak of a bird, as it burped the spirit into the tumbler. No-one in my family got very drunk. Getting smashed on a Friday night wasn't part of our culture. For all I knew, we could have harboured one or two inebriates. Yes, what about Granny's brothers? The one in the Navy, who was a bottle a day guy, whom she never liked to talk about?

With Lis' help, I changed into my black pencil skirt but when I put it on, it looked awful. She suggested I make the slit longer at the back and offered to do it with her nail scissors while I rummaged through the chest-of-drawers for a suitable blouse to wear. When I saw the white angora, I brought it out. Perfect! It would annoy Mum. She hated mohair and angora, believing they made the wearer look tarty. Mum preferred heathery shades, but not pastels, in sensible Botany wool.

Mum bristled with irritation as I entered the room. Afraid of her anger, I positioned myself as far from her as possible behind the winged chair by the fireplace and pretended to look at the oil painting Granny had given Mum, because she had recoiled at its subject: a prostitute standing in a brothel doorway next to a French café. The artist was Paul Maze, a French Impressionist. Granny knew him through his first wife whom he left for her cook. My grandmother never spoke to him again. In turn Maze demanded she return the three paintings of his that she possessed. Granny refused. Sotheby's had told her that Maze's work was valuable, but she wasn't persuaded to sell 'The French Café', the name she gave the painting. Neither would she hang on to it, given its unsavoury subject. So it went to Mum and Dad. Brothel or no brothel, the painting was worth something and that was all that mattered to them.

Clasping a silver salver that held several empty glasses, Mum approached me with a look of exasperation.

"What are you doing, Mary? Help me, for goodness sake!" she

complained, then turned smiling towards Chris, who was gazing in our direction. One reason Mum and Dad invited these young men to a slap-up meal, was to earn coinage for the time when we were old enough to be asked to their homes. I took over the salver. It was true, I hadn't helped Mum that day. Mrs Sykes was at the Infirmary because of her eye. I had read 'Bunty' upstairs all afternoon and discovered that if you beat up egg whites, mix them with honey and smear the mixture over your face, it would clean your skin and make it translucent.

"What's translucent?" Lis asked.

"It's what angels are like!"

"Just like you, I suppose!" she joked.

"It means 'shining through!" I tried to break up the word into Latin: 'Trans' was across and 'lucent' was shining."Remember to do your bust exercises!" reminded Lis. "Some people iron their hair but you'd better not. Mum'll go berserk." We settled for curling my eyelashes with a curler given to me by Marguerite who'd bought it in Marseille.

Mum wore a shapeless garment, neither tight nor full, that did nothing for her figure; she pinned Granny's gold brooch with seed pearls on it above her left breast.

As soon as Dad saw me in my black skirt, he said, "My, my, my. Mary, you look like a woman now!" Mum fiddled with the flower arrangement of winter jasmine and viburnum on the piano and nudged Dad in the ribs to make him realise he was pouring the drinks too large. I watched the scene from behind the winged chair. Chris was nearest and quite tall, five feet eleven inches. We were accustomed to height as Dad was six feet three. I didn't care for Chris's lips though. They were too thick and his Adam's apple, appeared and disappeared like a ping pong ball on the top of a diver's equipment. He was less stand-offish than Angus and Patrick, who stood around gawkily, pretending to be grown up.

"Have another!" Dad held up the bottle, splashing a quantity of sherry into Chris' glass. Mum had recovered her composure after my entrance and from her worries over Dad's generosity with the drinks. "How's your mother?" she asked Chris. "I always liked her.

At school she was far better at games than I was!"

I'd met Mrs Graddley, but couldn't imagine her playing a game of ping pong, let alone hockey or lacrosse. She was small and stout, although Daddy had called her plump. "She reminds me of a succulent Cox's orange!" Chris's Mum also had a voice that purred, her vowels sounding more Scottish than our parents'.

Chris looked at my Mum and jerked his head with a short, sharp movement that hinted at embarrassment. I couldn't work out if he was uneasy because of my nearness or because of Mum's memories of his mother.

"Well, now!" Dad announced, rubbing the palms of his hands together, "finish your drinks and we'll go and eat."

Dad liked eating too much. Not yet fifty he already had quite a paunch. Back in the kitchen, he stuck his head through the loops of an apron and tied the tapes round his back. Opening the oven door, he pulled out a tray with the roasting birds, basted them, and poured off the fat, for the remaining liquid to be made into gravy. As we gathered in the dining room, Dad read out from a crumpled piece of paper, the seating arrangements.

"Mary's next to Angus. Elisabeth, now where should you go? By Chris, I think. Patrick's next to...Janet and I forgot you, Esther! You're at the top of the table opposite me. And James just fits in there!" he pointed to a chair at the far side.

I entered the kitchen, to fetch dishes of peas and roast potatoes and when I returned, shot a furious look at Lis. How dare she sit next to Chris! Was she in cahoots with Dad? Was she going to steal him from me? She couldn't; she was only thirteen.

I watched them all.

Seated beside Chris was Patrick, who was laughing at Cara, growling at Pie, his Cocker spaniel, who was challenging her for her bone. Those men were a different species. I wondered if they had feelings like us. Did they bleed and cry and go to the loo? I could imagine Mum remonstrating with me. "Of course they do!" I'd never seen a man cry except once, or maybe twice. Dad lost control when he listened to Callas sing Mimi in 'La Boheme', with large tear-drops falling on to his moss-coloured jersey.

Mum carried the roast pheasants and pigeons into the dining room, placing them on a hot-plate on the side-board. Dad carved them. Hardly surgical in his method, he twisted and pulled the birds' limbs from the carcass, rather than cut directly through ligament or muscle. While Dad carved, donating a pheasant wing to a Duck Boy and a slice of breast for Mum, he maintained a skilful display of 'small talk'. "How's Edward's broiler birds?" he enquired of the poultry farm run by Patrick's father, or to James, "Is your father still rearing Jerseys?"

"Does he breed pullovers and jumpers as well?" asked Lis. Her wit impressed me but I was glad I didn't make the remark, risking ridicule and the Boys thinking me a silly girl. But everyone ignored what Lis said. Dad asked another question to keep up the conversation, as silence was an admission of social failure.

In their own turn, the Duck Boys. feigning maturity, offered to hand round the potatoes, bedded in a willow pattern dish and garnished with a sprig of mint. Chris took charge and with aplomb, let each person seated at the table, help themselves as he stood on their left, holding the dish out to them. I found this difficult, as I was left-handed and blushed when I dropped a potato; it rolled on to the floor beside his feet. I wondered if I should pick it up but if I did where could I put it? It was not hygienic to put it back on my plate. So I left it on the floor, disappointed that Chris had not been more helpful to me.

I could see Lis was watching every move I made. She waited for Chris to come round with the potatoes. When they arrived, she nestled into her chair, much like Mum's hens when they refused to budge from their nests, and slid the sleeves of her jumper up to her elbows. Where had she learned that? Not from Mum certainly. Daintily she picked up a potato, saying in a clipped, lady-like tone, "Thank you," without giving Chris a second glance. Yanking a drum stick from the carcass, Dad asked Chris if his father was still selling land to the Forestry Commission. "If you want my opinion, it's the best thing to do with rough ground!" Dad thrust the carving knife into the bird's belligerent fibres. "Let's not talk about that or Esther will be baying for my blood!"

Chris asked why, his query sounding so mature that Lis and I felt we were light years away from him in sophistication and experience.

"The Forestry Commission's sitka spruce, those horrible little fir trees, are like locusts, sucking up the soil's goodness," said Mum, letting a small potato drop from her fork to her plate. "Nothing lives in those awful woods," she said taking a handful of beans from Angus who had circled the table with his provender. Mum was wrong. We had seen foxes in the Forestry woods and up in the hills behind Newton Stewart, buzzards hovering over the road.

Dad sat on my right side and Angus, after he'd finished his round, returned to be on my left. I ate silently, agonising over what to say to him. I shouldn't have worried. All four Duck Boys were listening intently to Mum and Dad arguing over the Forestry Commission and whether it was a good thing. "They cause a terrible amount of flooding when they drain the land!"

"What else can it be used for?" was Dad's retort.

For a while, Angus said nothing; then he broke his silence. "Is it you who rides Loppy?" I nodded. I didn't want to be noticed for the one thing I took no pride in doing well. I rode because it was expected of me. That was all. He asked how much I fed my pony in winter and whether I jumped her in cross-country events. Pleased by Angus's attention, I began to lose my sense of shyness and told him more about Loppy, all her good points and faults.

"We had a horse once that always shied at water," he said.

I looked down at his plate. Finished eating his pheasant, Angus was tucking into a chipolata sausage.

"She cleared five barred gates but jibbed at water. Funny, isn't it?" Finishing his sausage, he laid his knife and fork on the plate and picked up his glass of wine, a South African Beaujolais, Dad said, "cheap but well chambré-ed, and if it's well chambré-ed, it's not so bad; at least one's guests think so."

Dad noticed immediately that Angus had finished eating. He leapt up to give his guest a second helping; moving to the hot plate, he pared more meat from the second pheasant. This was not an evening when he wished to be reminded of the parsimony forced on him. Many was the time he'd regale us with stories of pre-War opulence: of great covert shoots with pigeon, rabbit, pheasants, and partridges. Even snipe and woodcock. Now he was lucky to have a handful of pigeons and a brace of pheasants.

Angus's father had a grouse moor where he asked his friends to shoot with him on the Glorious Twelfth, but as Dad wasn't glorious enough to own one too, he was never invited.

Enjoying talking to Angus, I prayed for my chat with him to continue. I looked over the table at Lis to see if she'd noticed my accomplishment. She was eating in a persnickety way, a bit like Marguerite did last summer, and she looked bored, but that was not my problem. I'd got over my disappointment of not sitting next to Chris and I'd even begun to overlook Angus's frizzy hair and closely-set eyes.

"I say," he suggested, as the lemon mousse, Mum's dinner party staple, came round, "why don't you come and stay and we'll show you the course we do on our horses at home?"

I was amazed. Had Angus's invitation come through my scintillating conversation? Hardly! Maybe it was the beaten egg white that did it or the pencil slim skirt and angora jersey. It was like going fishing, skimming the fly over the water and catching one. Managing to attract a man, I basked in my new-found power and felt quite light-headed even though not one drop of the chambré-ed wine had touched my lips.

Dad rose from the table and walked to the cupboard below the window where he kept his alcohol, spirits mainly, along with bottles of brandy and port. Neither of my parents was interested in cocktails and mixers, although they served gin and French or Pimms' No 1 at cocktail parties in the summer.

He returned with a decanter of port and some small glasses.

His eyes met Mum's and she rose from her chair.

"Time to powder our noses!" she said to Lis and me. She had no intention of powdering her nose. I wondered why they stuck to this antiquated custom of us leaving the men to drink on their own, when we all knew the truth. She collected the empty pudding bowls and cream jug and carried them into the kitchen. With the door firmly shut, Mum quizzed me over Angus. Although at dinner, she'd argued vociferously with Dad about the Forestry Commission, she hadn't missed a thing.

"You mean, you've been asked to stay with the Mackenzies? That's quite a triumph! No one else in Wigtownshire has achieved that!" She looked at me in amazement.

"Shall I go and wipe the table?" I asked.

"Not now!" she said. "Leave the boys..."

"With their toys...." said Lis.

"I'll brush off the crumbs later and in the morning Mrs Sykes can polish the table properly," Mum told us. I helped her wash up. The pheasant carcass went into the big pot for soup and we laid aside the left-over vegetables for the dogs.

The Duck Boys stayed five days and shot six duck, three teal and two greylag. I couldn't understand why they enjoyed destroying birds, particularly the geese whose skeins, as they flew overhead, made such a hauntingly musical cry. Mum was ambiguous about wildfowlers. She even claimed that the sport was popular with bird lovers, an argument that made no sense. A few days after the Boys left, Mum received thank you letters from all four. Driving up to the back door, the postman handed us the first one in amongst a pile of brown envelopes. "Oh ae! There's quite a wee bundle there fer ye. Oh ae!" he repeated as he slammed shut the door of his van and drove away up the road, sloppy with cow dung. We scrutinised the post marks. "One from London, one from Glasgow, a tax bill, I think!" I wanted to show my younger sisters how much I knew about life, "and one from...Ayr. That's from a Duck Boy!"

I tried to stay calm and not let my sisters see how pleased I was he'd written. Angus wasn't my idea of a gorgeous man, but he served a purpose. He'd shown an interest in me and that was enough. "It's addressed to Mrs David Gladstone." I said.

"She's not called David; her name's Esther!" said Janet.

I agreed with her. Why call a woman by a man's name?

"When you marry you can lose your name!"

183

"Not your first one. Only your second," argued Lis.

"If that's the case, I'm not marrying!" Janet objected.

"Shall we steam it open?" I suggested.

We'd seen the process in a film where a mother steams open a letter sent to her daughter by a boy. This was the other way round. We'd be steaming open our Mum's letter from the boy. I grabbed the letter and went to the kitchen for the kettle but just then Mum entered from the back door, having fed her pullets.

"What are you doing?" she was suspicious. "Is that mine?"

Mum had a habit of tearing up her mail after reading it. If we weren't careful, we'd never get to read the letter. Looking cross, as if she'd not slept well, she followed us into the dining room with a plate of toast. We didn't ask why our Mum and Dad slept in separate beds for as long as we could remember, but they weren't particularly cuddly. Lis asked Dad why they weren't more a-ffectionate. Dad was offended and told her they were very good friends, and that's all they needed to be.

"There's a letter here, Mum!" I announced in a way that fooled no-one, least of all our Mum.

"Really, Darling?" She sat down heavily and shuffled the en-velopes as if they were a pack of cards. "That's interesting!" she studied the envelope with the Ayr postmark. then tore it open.

Trying not to appear too curious, I hummed the song Davina had played on her record player at Great White End at half term.

I even included the guitar sounds and all Buddy Holly's yoo hoos and chuckles. I didn't like him to look at, but I loved his voice and was about to move on to "Heartbeat" when Mum stretched an arm for the coffee pot on the table.

"Who's it from?"

"Angus!"

"What does he say?"

"The usual thing; just thank you."

"Anything else?"

"Not really, only he's going to Australia in two weeks time to work on a sheep station near Perth."

Angus paled into insignificance when, in the summer holidays, I met Mick and his father at the Wilsons. They had travelled up from Chipping Sodbury to fish for salmon on the River Luce. The following evening, Mick invited me to Shandalon, where a band played reels and although he didn't know how to dance any, except the 'eightsome', I guided him through 'Hamilton House' and 'The Reel of the 51st Division'. Mum made it her business to teach me simple steps like the 'pas de bas' for Scottish country dancing, so I wouldn't be a wallflower at social events. After Mick and I shuffled through the 'Gay Gordons', he suggested we leave the floor and step out the French window to smoke a cigarette. That's how it started, just like it often did in films. The man offers the woman a cigarette, which she accepts and while he holds his lighter to ignite it, they lean towards each other, and off they go. Neither of us thought we'd 'go all the way', but each hoped to get as close to it as possible. Anyway, we never found a time or place where we could do it.

The next day, when Lis saw me in my room, smiling into the mirror, as I applied 'coral pink' to my lips, she suspected something was up.

"Who's that for, then?"

"Nobody!"

"Come on!" she jeered. "Don't pull my leg! It's that boy you went to the reel party with. Mick, isn't that his name?"

"It might be!"

"There you are!" she nudged me in the ribs. "When can we see him? Is he nice? Nicer than Angus, I hope!"

"I think so. Actually, I know so."

"I hope his Adam's apple doesn't go biddly, biddly boing like Chris' did. And he can't have spots? Tell me he has none!"

"No-oo?"

I didn't want to tell her, but he did. Quite a few on his forehead and on the end of his nose. But I didn't mind. They weren't as bad as my cousin's had been. When I asked Mum if he still had them, she said they'd all disappeared. So, I supposed Mick's would too. After I finished with my lipstick, I took a look at myself. I looked good, wearing Davina's hand-me-down velveteen slacks and her turquoise blouse with the plunging neckline.

"Where are you going? Lis asked.

"Nowhere! Mick's coming for supper here!"

I liked him. More importantly, I could now boast in having a boyfriend, something most girls my age in Wigtownshire could not do. On our last evening together, Mick gave me a bottle of Christian Dior eau de toilette. When Mum saw it standing on my dressing table, she scoffed.

"Scent? At your age? Ridiculous! Only townees wear that! It's just..." she couldn't find the right word. Neither Mum, Douna nor any of her friends would dream of wearing it. They competed with each other to be the worst-dressed and least sexy woman in the country.

"What's wrong with wearing scent or perfume or whatever you like to call it?" I asked. She didn't need to explain. I knew; to her it was unnecessary and too girly.

Mick and I promised to write every other day and to telephone, although his parents forbade him to speak to anyone for more than three minutes at a time. A brief distraction from my new passion was the arrival of my GCE O level results. I picked up the envelope, that had fallen dangerously close to the dogs' water bowl at the back door but hesitated to open it.

"Go on, Mary!," urged Mum. "Just do it! Pretend you're on Loppy, throwing caution to the wind and, well, you know...get on with it. Jump! Throw yourself over the bar!"

I tore open the envelope and read out my results. Exam papers were marked out of 9. The top mark was 1, the bottom, 9. Everything from 1 to 6, was a pass. "English lit, 3, English lang 5, History 3, Latin 2, Art 5, Biology 3 and French 3. I'd passed them all, not with flying colours but I'd done alright.

The phone rang. I wasn't interested in who it was but Mum rushed into the other room to answer it.

"Of course!" I heard her say through the door. "When would you like them to come?"

"Oh, no!" Lis groaned. "Someone wants us for a stupid meal at their house."

"Lunch at 12.30! Wonderful!" said Mum. "They'll love that. Thank you so much!"

"Who is it this time!" asked Lis, as Mum came back into the room. Neither Lis nor Janet liked going to the homes of Mum's friends. They preferred to stay at Carsenestock to be with the Marrs, who went net fishing on the Cree below the farm. When they saw them draw up at the farm, they'd rush down to the inks in their wellingtons. At the end of the day, my sisters sat with the family in their car, drinking tea from a thermos flask and daring each other to smoke one or two of the Marrs' cigarettes.

"It's Veronica Houghton!" Mum announced. "She's up from London with Prudence and Judith. They're staying with their Aunt Edwina and Uncle Philip.

"What do they want?"

"For you to lunch with them at Lochwilly."

"OK!" said Lis grudgingly, "but I'm coming back home by four o'clock. The Marrs said they were turning up then."

The next day, Mum drove us to Judith and Prudence, who was my age, give or take a year. Like me, she was tall and not slim. She attended a girls' boarding school in Dorset and played the clarinet. She said that at the end of the following term, she then would 'come out', meaning she'd be launched into 'polite' society.

"I'll wear a long white dress and go to lots of London balls. Maybe even come up to Scotland and go to some more."

"Oh!" was my succinct reply.

"In the old days, when you came out, you were presented to the Queen!" she said.

"Oh!"

"I'm going to be a deb!"

"Oh!"

"Deb's short for debutante!"

I knew what it meant. 'Debut' in French meant 'the beginning'. So she'd be a beginner, but in what? A certain kind of life, I supposed. Judith, closer in age to Lis, had other desires. "I'm going to RADA to train to be an actress!" I was about to say 'Oh!' again but thought better of it. Unlike her older sister, Judith had ambition and would, I was certain, fulfil it, just as Peter, the Rintouls' son, asserted he'd be a millionaire by the time he was thirty.

The sisters' aunt and uncle lived in a wooden house, built in world war one as a hospital for wounded soldiers. After lunch, we left the adults to play ping pong in a summer house in the garden. We soon tired of the game and had a go at playing darts instead. On a low table by the board was a stack of glossy, very old magazines. Judith bent down to scrutinise them. Flicking through the pages. She paused at one showing a full-length photographic studio portrait of a young woman.

"Ooooooh!" she cried in mock appreciation. "Miss Millicent Fortescue Grundy! Isn't she awful! Look at her hair! It's in really tight waves like the corrugated cardboard wrapped around china when it's sent in the post. And those thin lips. She looks like a stuck-up, snooty..." I peered at the photograph. Judith wrenched the magazine from me. She was in full flood: "So, what's she in the magazine for? Ooooh! She's about to get married."

"Who to?" asked Prudence. "We might know them."

"Mr Telford Whitney of Gropen Lodge, Olney, Buckingham-shire.

"No, I have never heard of them, but Mummy might,." said Prudence.

Judith chucked away the magazine and picked up another. "Here's another lady, if you can call her that. And her claim to fame is she's getting married too. To another twit!"

"Don't you want to get married?" Prudence asked of her sister.

"I don't care! I just want to go on the stage!"

"Don't you know what Noel Coward said about that?"

"Mrs Worthington's daughter was fat and ugly. I'm the very opposite!"

I had to admit, Judith wasn't lying, or over-confident about her looks. She was fabulously pretty and very sexy in spite of what Mum thought of women and girls like that. I suspected she was relieved that none of us was as stunning to look at as Judith.

"Well, I'm quite ordinary, I'm afraid," admitted Prudence. "I want to marry and have children; two boys and a girl, and live in a large-ish house."

Did I want that? I was unsure. The future stretched before me like an empty plain, similar to the sand dunes in Lawrence of Arabia, which I'd just seen with Mick when he took me to the showing in Newton Stewart.

Judith tore out of the magazine the page of Millicent Fortescue Grundy, pinned it on to the wall beside the dart board, and threw a dart. "Got her right between the eyes! Look!"

"Oh, you are silly!" protested Prudence before she grabbed a dart and flung it at Millicent's right eye. Let's see if I can get her in the left one too!" She hurled another at the picture.

It wasn't long before all of us were seizing magazines, tearing out pages featuring beautiful, young women from long ago, and pinning them to the wall, and throwing darts at them. When Veronica, Prudence and Judith's mother, entered the summer-house, she gasped at our ritual carnage.

"Oh dear!" she exclaimed in feigned horror. "How could you? Poor Millicent, she was deb of my year. Not Julia, you couldn't! You know, her Jonathan was killed in the Normandy landings and as for Jane, you haven't attacked her too? She went downhill quite rapidly and took to the bottle, poor thing.. Who could blame her when she was stuck with that rat, Eddie Pringle Watt? Oh well, at least you've found a use for them and for yourselves!" she laughed. "Tea's ready! Come in before you massacre the whole lot of them!"

It seemed to me that time had already done that.

Soon after, like all the others in my class at Badminton, I was summoned for a talk with BMS about my future. She sat in her carpeted study on her swivel chair and looked me straight in the eye. "Well, now, Mary!"

I knew from experience that this preamble didn't mean she was particularly pleased with my recent academic performance.

She held out few hopes for me as I wasn't one of her chosen few. "Congratulations on your O level results. Your Latin was rather good." I didn't dare tell her that the reason for the high mark was because I had learned by heart before the exam the entire English translation of the set passages. "You've worked hard in some areas of your studies, especially your report on Georgian Bristol." I'd done this to impress Dad. As a qualified architect, he loved the Georgian period, whether in London, Bath, Bristol or Edinburgh. When I showed him my efforts though, he wasn't particularly interested.

"When all things are considered, Mary," explained BMS, "I wouldn't recommend you study English for Advanced level, nor French or History and for that reason, I don't think you should apply for university. I suggest instead that you spend a term at a school in France. I know a good one near Lyon.

Well, why not, I thought. It might be nice, but I left her room with a defiant thought: I'll show you. Maybe not this year or the next, but one day, Brenda Mary Sanderson, I'll show you.

I SET OFF from Waterloo on the Dover train for my French school. On the boat, I met a teacher who had booked us a room in a Paris hotel before we caught a train south to Lyon the next morning. France was the only country I wanted to visit, as I already spoke a little French, enough to say good morning, how are you, where's the toilet/railway station/ baker's shop or library. My aim was to be fluent in the language by the end of the term. Collège Cévenol, my new school, was situated on the outskirts of Le Chambon-sur-Lignon in France's south-central Haute-Loire region.

I didn't know it then, that I was about to stay in a remarkable French village. Since the seventeenth century, Le Chambon-sur-Lignon's residents were Huguenots (Protestants), their rebellious origins influencing the villagers' actions during world war two. Protestant ministers, André Trocmé and Edouard Theis, who founded College Cévenol in 1938, were leaders of a movement of residents who risked their lives by hiding Jewish people on farms, in private houses, and public institutions. When Nazi patrols arrived in the village, the inhabitants led the fugitives into the mountains, then hailed them out of hiding by singing a special song. By 1942 the situation became more tense as Germany invaded France's South Zone, but village residents continued to protect Jews by providing them shelter, forging identity and ration cards, and helping some, perhaps 1,000 or 5,000, to cross into neutral Switzerland. No one kept track. Records were dangerous.

Not everyone in the family was enthusiastic about my visit. While Mum and Dad were trying to decide whether I should go, Granny wrote and warned them of the dangers I might meet.

When it came to young English women and French men, Granny was Franco-phobic. I don't think Mum knew that when Iris, Granny's youngest sister, stayed in fin de siècle Paris, her host had, in Granny's words, 'tried to take advantage' of her. Perhaps, she herself was seduced by a French man or pestered and stalked by another. At any rate, she was sufficiently suspicious of the Gallic approach to want me warned about French men. She wouldn't like anything to happen to "pretty blue-eyed Mary", she wrote. I was surprised by her concern and how affectionate she sounded on paper. What put the wind up her, I'm sure, was that I would be a pupil at a mixed boarding school, something she was more suspicious of.

I panicked when no-one met me on the boat, but as I disembarked to wait on the pier, a woman approached holding a placard with' Collège Cévenol' written on it.

Three others accompanied us: a girl from Buckinghamshire and two boys from the West country. When we reached Paris, we boarded a taxi which drove us to a hotel at La Gare Austerlitz. The next day, after our petit déjeuner, we prepared for the next stage of our journey, this time by train. A little apprehensive but hardly homesick, I was accustomed to long train journeys. On a cold, January morning, we left Paris, heading for Lyon and arrived there in the early evening. As we waited outside the station for our coach to arrive and drive us to the school, an American boy approached me.

"Hi, there!" he said. "My name's Ben. What's yours?"
"Mary!"
"Are you English?" he asked.
"Not quite! I'm half and half. English and Scots."
"That's interesting! I was in Scotland last summer. We stayed with an English girl and her father. Maybe you know her!"

I looked at him, thinking he was not only naïve but mad. The UK might be small by comparison to the USA, but it had a large population. Didn't he know?

"Her name's Polly Toynbee!"

My jaw dropped. "Yes," I said, annoyed I couldn't show him up for his naivety. "She was at school with me." I refrained from adding that she did a nice line in organizing conferences on sensitive political issues. Ben's mother and Polly's father were old friends, it turned out. Ben met Polly when the two families stayed at Inch Kenneth, an island off Mull on Scotland's west coast. From the way he talked about Polly, I could tell he was quite taken with her. I was taken with Ben, but soon learned a lot of girls were.

On arriving at the school, a matron showed me the dormitory, which I was to share with two others: Françoise, who soon told me that last term she'd been Ben's girlfriend, but this term he decided not to be involved with her; he preferred solitude and maybe even to write a novel. The other occupant was Marie Christine who, because of my lapse in the language, only associated with Francoise. They guzzled food each night sent from home: macaroons, chocolate cake, large bars of Lindt chocolate, and other goodies, but seldom shared them with me.

It was little wonder that my dormitory companions received food parcels. Most students at the Collège did. Collège Cévenol hardly went in for French gastronomy; the food there was awful, much worse than what we ate at Badminton School. Never a keen carnivore, I suspected that some of it was horse meat. Neither could I abide sweetmeats like brains, heart, or tripe. What really put me off was the fish. It tasted odd. I assumed that because the upper Loire was a long way from the sea, we had to eat fresh-water fish: carp, perch or bream. Accustomed to haddock, cod or whiting, I couldn't acclimatize to the fresh-water variety. Neither could I bear seeing it on the plate with its head and tail on and often with the roe still inside. So, for most of the term, I ate chips, potatoes, and white bread.

Collège Cévenol was primarily for French children who had failed to pass into the standard French Lycée system. Most, therefore, were desperate to pass their Baccalauréat, which to us Anglo-Saxons seemed impossibly rigorous. Because the French had to swot and do homework each evening, we foreigners fell back on each other for recreation and company, which defeated the very purpose of coming to the school: to learn French.

Much of the upper Loire was wooded and mountainous. The village itself was still a Protestant stronghold, its church resembling the Presbyterian kirk in Scotland. Just as at Penninghame at the end of the school term, we'd file into St. John's, Newton Stewart, to listen to the minister rant from the pulpit, each and every Sunday morning we'd attend 'le culte', a religious service. When I gained more confidence, I'd truant whenever I could.

The Collège's teachers were religious and dedicated. Monsieur Cordonnier, introduced us to Racine, Corneille and Victor Hugo but not, understandably, Rimbaud, Verlaine, Baudelaire and the infamous Villon. Monsieur Cordonnier was perhaps the very first teacher of genius I'd come across. He showed us how a poet of one nation can describe an event completely differently from another, depending upon the outcome. Reciting the second stanza of Victor Hugo's 'L'Expiation', "Waterloo, Waterloo, Waterloo, morne plaine, Comme une onde qui bout dans une urne trop pleine!", our teacher demonstrated how words, in the sounds they made, can conjure up mood and atmosphere. Certainly Hugo's lament, written after Napoleon's defeat at Waterloo, is unequivocally mournful. But I associated Waterloo with triumph. In English at Badminton, Miss Franklin introduced us to Robert Browning's interpretation: 'How they Brought the Good News from Ghent to Aix': "I sprang to the stirrup, and Joris and he; I galloped, Dirck, galloped, we galloped all three."

Not to be outdone, a sweet old Spanish teacher also taught us well, with warmth and affection, and would dismiss us at the end of each class with, "Et maintenant, vous pouvez aller libres comme les oiseaux!" or "And now you go free like birds."

History classes were an eye-opener; at Badminton we studied Robert Peel, Gladstone and Disraeli; Collège Cèvenol focused on nineteenth century French, Italian and Austrian political figures. The teacher didn't make things easy. She stood at the front of the class, disgorging dozens of dates and names.

Judging from the frequency with which Dreyfus and Cavour cropped up, I guessed they were important. I hadn't heard of either. From what I gathered, Alfred Dreyfus, a Jewish captain in the French army was wrongly accused of treason but eventually pardoned. Our teacher flagged him up because, as a Huguenot stronghold, the Collège and Le Chambon-sure-Lignon knew all about scapegoating and discrimination. When it came to Cavour, his role was simple: as an Italian noble and statesman, he was the leading figure in the movement towards his country's Unification.

In January, a statesman, this time of a noble, English family, hit the headlines. Winston Churchill died. Madame La Ronde, who was in charge of the girls' boarding house, pulled me aside with tears in her eyes, "Nous n'oublions jamais, Monsieur Churchill!" "We never forget," she said emphatically. "Pendant la guerre, nous écoutions à sa voix." or "During the war, we listened to his voice."

I lost the rest of what she said, but I listened to a recording of Churchill's war-time radio speeches to occupied France after that, and Madame, who usually ignored me, asked me into her room to watch Churchill's state funeral on television. I'm ashamed to admit that I'd rather have gone to the village to meet my friends or sit in the café and eat a patisserie, but Madame's desire to pamper me, with hot chocolate, and tartines with anchovy paste, had me watching the spectacle but ignoring the French commentary, as I barely understood a word.

Madame was not so pleasant when I received a telegram from Mick. Coincidentally, he'd come to France at the same time as me to work near Tours in a vineyard. We wrote to each other regularly and arranged a clandestine meeting one weekend. Granny should have been more concerned about expatriate Englishmen in France than the actual residents themselves, but at the last moment, Mick cried off; possibly a wise move as we had nowhere to stay.

He sent me a telegram, that included his surname. Madame read it and quizzed me about the name. "Quesque c'est ce nom MORGAN?" she asked.

She let it pass but from then on, although I was Mr. Churchill's compatriot, she no longer trusted me.

I didn't want Mick to win the day, so I arranged instead to stay the weekend in Lyon with Mlle Vignier who kindly invited me. An old friend of Helen Drew, who attended Challoch church, dressed like a man, and whose mother counted her small change during the sermon, would have to do. Planning to take a train, I discovered that Ben was also traveling north, hitch-hiking as far as Paris. He asked if I wanted to go some of the way with him.

I said yes, partly to annoy Francoise by telling her about the trip when I returned. While waiting by the roadside for a lift, Ben told me that his mother was the English writer, Jessica Mitford.

"Then your aunt is Nancy!" I said amazed.

"Yes! Have you read her books?" he asked. "I haven't. I've read my mother's, though."

" I've read all of them!" I answered. 'The Pursuit of Love' and 'Love in a Cold Climate''. The strange, aristocratic family of neglected girls, who loved their animals more than their parents, fascinated me, obviously, but whereas Nancy translated her child-hood experiences into fiction, Jessica kept them as fact. Ben told me that Polly Toynbee's father, Philip, had been a university friend of Esmond Romilly, Jessica's first husband, who died in the War.

"I refuse to read Nancy's on principle!" Ben laughed.

"Will you look her up in Paris? Doesn't she live there?"

But he didn't say. A pick-up van with a silent farmer, carting sheep to the market, stopped for us. He deposited us at a field near a village. We then thumbed a lift in a lorry. Ben tried to engage the driver in conversation. He was far better at French than me and had picked up dozens of colloquialisms and a lot of slang.

Having him ask me to hitch-hike with him was quite a coup and I couldn't wait to tell my room-mate, the petite, brown-eyed, pretty Françoise, who still pined for him. She often repeated his name after lights out, "Ben a fait un..." or "Ben était tout..." or "Ben me plaisait..." or "Ben va...." I couldn't help but smirk at the thought and wanted to tell her "Ben is with me and not with you! or "maintenant, Ben est avec moi et pas avec toi, Françoise!" and I would have added in French, if I could, "and lardy boo sucks to you, Missy", but it was beyond me. If I didn't understand what Françoise was saying about him, I knew from the tone of her voice and the way she repeated his name that she still wanted him.

In the lorry, I sat close to Ben so the driver wouldn't touch my leg when he changed gear. I liked the feel of my companion's body, the sense of his breath, and the way the sleeve of his jacket brushed against my hand. But I knew we wouldn't get together, apart from the fact that I was still with Mick.

Ben wanted to spend his time alone, though most of the term he'd already been closeted in his room. I suspected he wanted to emulate his mother and aunt by writing a novel.

In order not to be too late for my rendez-vous with Mlle Vignier, we caught a train for the final stage of the journey.

When we met at the railway station in Lyon, Ben came into his own. "Permettez , Madamoiselle, nous offrir nos regrettes..."

"Nous sommes en retard!" I added, remembering how to say that we're late in French.

"Nous avons eu un pan d'auto!" Ben said. Blaming a problem with the car was a whopping, big lie but told with such charm, he got away with it. Enchanted by the ease with which Ben spoke her language, Mlle Vignier congratulated him.

"He's learned it well!" she said as she drove me away to her apartment. Her niece, Babette, lived with her, the old lady complained. I only understood some of her instructions, "ne jette pas le savon dans la poubelle" and "il faut laver les bas chaque soir". Nobody had ever told me not to throw the soap away or to wash my stockings each evening! It never occurred to me to do it, as Mum didn't recommend we keep our clothes in order. At Badminton, we'd shoved our dirty linen into laundry bags. Each house had its own color; mine was sage green. Admittedly, Mum had clothed us well but not neatly or prettily. She took the trouble, however, to knit us jumpers and cardigans, supply cord trousers and aertex shirts and always made us wear our hair short.

Weeks later Jessica, Ben's mother visited Le Chambon-sur-Lignon and a group of us met her in the village pâtisserie. Looking every bit an aristocratic lady in her immaculate tweed suit, a coat and skirt, she appeared slim, elegant and very English. but I was too shy to speak to her. Ben invited me but once there, I was tongue-tied. He'd asked us to meet his mother outside the school. Perhaps he'd realized, as I had, that there were few people he wished to converse with there. I hadn't met anyone either who I felt an affinity with, apart from M. Cordonnier, the gentle, old Spanish teacher and a few American students like Jeff, who was friendly and talkative but not very tall. I discussed politics with him and learned about Democrats and Republicans. Jeff also alerted me to the significance of individual skin colour. "One day we'll all be the same," he said. "Khaki!"

I didn't agree with his American idea of a melting pot. I liked it that we were all different: white, black, brown or yellow.

"You don't know about race problems!" he said. "When you're black or otherwise in America, you have a shit life! If you're a WASP —"

He saw my bemused expression.

"White Anglo-Saxon Protestant!" he said.

It was early 1965 and we were on the eve of a social revolution, but we didn't know that yet.

Sometimes I'd explore the village in the snow, which lay deep on the ground. People who knew, said conditions for skiing were excellent at Le Chambon-sur-Lignon. Our instructor was away. I borrowed a pair of skis and tried to learn myself but didn't. I met friends at the village Pâtisserie. The cakes looked better than they tasted, but their names were fine: chocolate éclairs, meringues, les religieuses, rhum babas, and extravagant slices of gâteau. The cream wasn't cream as I knew it but a disappointingly flavoured custard or 'crême anglaise'. That the French called anything un-authentic and unappealing English, Spanish or Italian, amused me.

If I had nothing else to do, I'd walk through the village up into the countryside across fields, down lanes and into the woods. One morning I missed "Le Culte". I never understood the sermons anyway and tramped off up a hill. I didn't fear I'd be accosted. I never was. This part of France was sober, upright and God-fearing. On one unusually bright morning, I felt exceptionally alive. It was a brief moment of feeling invincible. I continued on, crunching through the snow in magical boots. Nothing could stop me, not even my regret that I still couldn't speak good French.

As the lane sank into a decline, I approached a foot-bridge crossing a stream and found myself wading knee-deep in the snow. Everything seemed wonderful and life was opening up perfectly before my eyes. Nothing could go wrong and Mick could go to hell. I didn't want him anyway. He was far too conventional. The only cloud on the horizon was I had no idea what I wanted to do with my life. But on that morning, in this amazing world, I was full of hope. I'd find my way. All I wanted was to be me: young, healthy and curious. I was reminded of that young adder I'd seen as a child waking from its sleep one sunny, spring morning. I tramped up a slope, arriving at a village with a shop, I pushed the door open and asked at the counter for a bar of chocolate.

"Voilà Madame!" said the owner. Madame? He called me Madame! Did I look that grownup?

I was happy when the term ended. My stomach suffered from my poor diet, I had learned little French, and had felt very lonely at times when people ignored me. On the plus side I'd enjoyed listening to the sardonic tones of the Belgian singer, Jacques Brel. I had met a few interesting people though, but I couldn't say my term at Collège Cévenol was an unmitigated success. To cap it all, Diana, the English girl from Buckinghamshire, and a good friend during the term, moved to a different compartment so she could snog with one of the West country boys on the overnight train from Lyon to Paris.

I was never more happy than when I said goodbye to them on the boat from Calais and saw the white cliffs of Dover.

I wondered deeply what would meet me on returning home, but I knew now I'd have my own portrait. I'd crawled out from under the family rock to a new light, away from the underside of innocence. Crossing the Channel, I was above a border, looking all ways.

Gladstones

```
                    Thomas of Leith = Helen Neilson
                       1732-1809        1739-1806

Sir John                          (Bob) Robert = Catherine
 1764-1851                          1773-1835

William Ewart   Helen        (Tom) Thomas
1809-1898       1814-1880     1805-1882
                              Samuel Steuart
                              1837-1909
                              (1887-1949) Sir Hugh = Cecil, sister of Constance Sitwell
                                                         (Aunt Conty)

John = Louise    Jean = Roderick Barclay   David=Esther      Jim=Rosamund Fellowes
1908-1977              (Uncle Roddie)           Macdonald         (div)
                                                                  Jamie

Davina  Joe    Mary  Lis  Janet  Colin
```

The Macdonalds

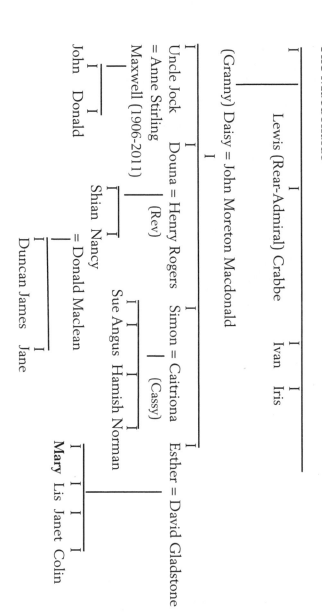

Lewis (Rear-Admiral) Crabbe

Ivan   Iris

(Granny) Daisy = John Moreton Macdonald

Uncle Jock   Douna = Henry Rogers   Simon = Caitriona   Esther = David Gladstone
= Anne Stirling   (Rev)   (Cassy)
Maxwell (1906-2011)

John   Donald

Shian   Nancy   Sue Angus Hamish Norman
         = Donald Maclean

Duncan James   Jane

Mary Lis Janet Colin

Friends and Neighbors

Mum's and Granny's friends

Margaret Spicer, Mum's school-friend
Alan Whitehorn, Mum's friend from before the War
Margaret Mackenzie, Mum's war-time friend and my godmother
Dorothea Russell, friend of Daisy (Granny)
Mary Anne O'Malley (Ann Bridge) friend of both grandmothers

Local Friends and Neighbors

Helen Drew
Sir Aymer Maxwell and nephew, Michael
Major Michael Cliff McCulloch
The Buchan-Hepburns
Elizabeth Campbell-Paisley
Veronica Houghton
Enoch Patrick
Dr Sampson

Mum's Cousins

Bride Binney
Winifred Hayter

Mary's Friends

Margaret Kyle
Melanie Fraser
Julia Clarke
Prudence and Judith
Mick Morgan, Mary's boyfriend
American Jeff (slightly left-wing)

Mary's Unattainable Friends

Angus Mackenzie (hived off to Perth, Australia)
Polly Toynbee (too clever and famous)
Katherine Whitehorn (same as above)
Ben Treuhaft (too solitary, attractive and popular)

Time-Line

Aged 4 ½   Move from south-east England
                         to south-west Scotland.
Aged 5   Queen's visit to Newton Stewart (1953)
Aged 5   Enter primary school
Aged 6   Incident in granary
Aged 6   Birth of brother
Aged 9   Incident with school bus driver
Aged 9   Visit to Granny, Anne and Aunt Caitriona
Aged 9   the Chase
Aged 9½   Interview at Badminton School
Aged 10   Enter Badminton School, Bristol
Aged 15   Supper with Duck Boys
Aged 16   Meet Mick, my first boyfriend
Aged 16½   Leave Badminton School
Aged 16½   Enter College Cevenol
Aged 16¾   Return home

Penninghame School, Newton Stewart

Primary 1   (5 yrs- 6 yrs)   Mrs Gillanders
Primary 2   (6 yrs –7 yrs)   Miss Field
Primary 3   (7 yrs – 8 yrs)   Mrs Dunlop
Primary 4   (8 yrs- 9 yrs)   Mr Godfrey
Primary 5   (9 yrs – 10 yrs)   Mrs Trotter

Au Pairs and Other Helpers

Anna
Martha
Helga
Dora
Pat
Mrs Sykes